From Out House
to Outer Space

Ed. D. Jones

ISBN 0-7414-3949-2

Published by:

INFI∞ITY
PUBLISHING.COM

1094 New DeHaven Street, Suite 100
West Conshohocken, PA 19428-2713
Info@buybooksontheweb.com
www.buybooksontheweb.com
Toll-free (877) BUY BOOK
Local Phone (610) 941-9999
Fax (610) 941-9959

Printed in the United States of America

Printed on Recycled Paper

Published October 2007

I dedicate this book to:

My Mother; Georgia Alice Farnham Jones Chilcott.

My lovely Wife of 50 plus years; Catherine Sylvia Smith Jones. A constant companion. Thank you for being there.

Our three Sons; Ed Wilmot, Brian Derward and Gary Philip Jones. And their wife's, Linda, Rebecca and Janice who are like daughters to us.

Our grandchildren; Cody, Alyssa, Chad, Logan and Chaney Jones

Renee Logsdon and Kaydee Jones who chose to adopt Cathy and me as GrandMa and GrandPa, and to those that choose to call us Mom and Dad; Robyn Logsdon, Ed and Carol Hadle.

Our good friends Richard and Betty Geiger who cared enough to travel with us to California for our fiftieth wedding celebration.

Dr. Donald Swanson D. D. S. for encouraging me to write the story of my life.

The many true and faithful friends that touched our lives and those who guided me along life's journey in my youth.

PROLOGUE

I learned very early that life's journey is not always easy, but with a positive attitude and belief in the LORD life will only be a challenge. All the challenges will tend to make you stronger. As long as you keep trying you can reach your goals.

The greatest loss that I see is that the youth of today will never know the pain and suffering of their parents and grandparents. They have only text books to learn from and not the history from living persons.

The greatest reward I have learned from my journey is the love of and from family and friends.

INDEX

CHAPTER ONE

THE EARLY DAYS

My parents Ed Wilmot Jones and Georgia Alice were married November 23, 1920.

I (Ed Derward Jones) was born October 17, 1924 in Selma, California to Georgia Alice Farnham Jones and Ed Wilmot Jones. My sister Georgia Lee Jones was born August 7, 1922 in Oklahoma. We were the best of friends our entire life and supported each other. I always thought she was the prettiest girl I had ever seen. We spent lots of good times together. Mom and Dad took us every where they went. Mom often told me about sitting on her lap while Dad was driving their 1st car. It was a striped down Model T Ford. There were no doors on it. Dad made a left turn and Mom thought he was going to turn right. She slid off kerplunk on the ground with me still sitting on her lap.

We often went to see Grandma and Grandpa Farnham in Porterville, CA. for holidays and some times just to visit. We had to go through Strathmore, which is a small farm town nestled in the foot hills of the Sierra Nevada Mountains. This was where they would often stop and take pictures. Thus the picture of Georgia Lee when she was just 1 year old.

Georgia Lee Jones 1 yr old

Grandma and Grandpa Farnham

Grandma and Grandpa Farnham purchased 5 acres in Porterville. It had no barn so they had to milk their cow out in the open, come rain or shine. Grandpa built a small chicken house for the few chickens they had. There was no running water or bathroom in the house. At onetime a slough ran through the property about 300 feet behind the house. On the edge of the slough is where the out house was. It always had a Sears or Montgomery Ward catalogue next to the seat to look at and use pages as toilet paper.

I got to see Grandma and Grandpa quite often. I was about 6 months old when it was decided that we should go visit Dad's parents in Hot Springs, New Mexico. They were well established there and had a house made of home made adobe blocks. It was a very long trip from California to New Mexico for Georgia Lee and me and we let it be known loud and clear.

Grandma Jones

Grandpa Jones

Grandma and Grandpa Jones moved to Hot Spring for the mineral water. The Mineral Springs made a small pool where Chief Geronimo went and took some of his braves with him. They were seen there quite often in the days long before my time. Grandma and Grandpa opened the first public Hot Mineral Springs bathhouse in the town. I of course had to have a mineral bath. It was rumored that Grandma was Cherokee Indian. Grandpa and his brothers were known as the best cattle counters in the country. They could look a herd of cattle and estimate how many there were.

From New Mexico, we went to Yuma Arizona where Dad got a job as a carpenter. Dad built the home we lived in by himself. I remember sitting between my mom and dad in the 1924 Dodge. My sister was on Mom's lap. One time while I was still in diapers Mom took me outside and sat me down under a tree in the shade. Next thing she knew I was screaming as loud as I could. Mom ran out to see what the problem was and discovered she had sat me down right on top of a big red ant bed. She picked me up, brushed the ants off and took me inside. She knew I liked oat meal so she made a bowl for me and put more sugar on it than usual. I chewed very slowly, not fast like usual so she got the sugar out and put more on it. I chewed even slower so she called to Georgia Lee and told her to taste it. Georgia Lee took a big mouth full and made an ugly face. Mom asked what was wrong and Georgia Lee said it was too salty. Mom discovered that she had been putting salt on instead of sugar.

Early on the morning of my third birthday I looked out the window and saw my sister. I called to Mom and said "see now I'm taller than her." I went outside and found out how wrong I was. I had not sprouted over night. I remember my Dad at church outside in the yard. He was kneeling on his right knee with his left leg bent. He was talking to other men. I had to copy him and kneel down like him including putting a piece of straw in my mouth.

Dad often made ice cream while Mom, Georgia Lee and I played hide and go seek in the field behind our house. We often went on a picnic in the sand dunes not far from our home. We had to drive over the railroad ties that were held together with metal strips. The road was built out of railroad ties as the sand shifted a lot when the wind blew. The highway construction department had not figured out how to make a permanent road in the sand hills. If you met a car coming from the opposite direction the drivers would work together, moving one car off the road so the other one could go by. After the car had passed the drivers would put the car that was in the sand back on the road.

One day I had a nickel and asked Mom to take me to the store but she said she couldn't as Dad had the keys I went out side to where Dad was digging a well and said "Mom needs the car keys" Dad tossed me the keys without asking a question. Mom looked out the window when she heard the car running and saw the car backing out of the drive way. It was jerking like it wasn't running very good and she saw no one driving. She ran out to the car, opened the door and saw me on the floor working the clutch and brake peddles with my hands. Some how I had gotten the car started and in reverse gear. I had always watched as Dad drove the car and knew he pushed the peddles with his feet but I couldn't reach them with my feet so I tried my hands. How I ever got it started and in gear I'll never know.

At Christmas time Mom and Dad would visit their friends with gifts to exchange. They would visit several different families and this was exciting for Georgia Lee and me as we would not only receive small gifts but would play with the children. Neat playing with so many children, most around our age.

I had a dog name Lightening, I called him Lightnen Miffin Muffen Jones. I liked muffins which I called miffin muffens and I liked my dog. I played a lot with my good old dog. One day he started walking down the street and I followed him a short distance before Mom caught up with me. She scolded Lightening for leaving the yard but did not get angry with me, only explained that even if the dog walked in the street it was too dangerous for me because people in cars could not see me and I couldn't get out of the way fast like my dog.

Dad, Lightnen Muffin Jones and me

Big old pants

One of my early memories is that like all young children I was dressed in rompers or a dress. I was probably around 18 months old when Mom bought me a shirt and my first pair of pants. I called them my big old pants. I was so proud of them I had Mom help me walk next door to show Al and Josie White. Mrs. White made out like they were the best pants ever made. She then offered me a drink of water without rinsing the glass. I poured the water out and asked her to rinse the glass then get me some fresh water. She looked at me kind of funny and asked my mother if I always did that? I suppose I learned it at home, we probably all drank out of the same glass at home and rinsed it every time we used it. We spent one night at the Whitefields. They had beds outside for the children as it was cooler than in the house. I told Mom that I didn't want my big old pants to get wrinkled. She showed me how to fold them and said, "If I put them under the mattress they would be pressed in the morning." She also put a hair clip in my hair so I would have the wave in it that I wanted kind of a pompadour. Dad used to take us to the local swimming pool. He taught me to swim before I was able to walk and I had a lot of fun swimming with him.

We went to my Grandparents house in California for thanksgiving. There were lots of Aunts, Uncles and cousins there. I must have been a show off as I liked to prance around in my big old pants. I learned that I could curl my toes under and walk on my toe knuckles. I would do this every time some one was looking at me. Uncle Jack Turney put me on his knee and taught me to say, "Once I was a little boy upon my father's knee, but now I am a big boy fit to serve the king. I can hold a musket and I can smoke a pipe and I can kiss a pretty girl at twelve o'clock at night." Every one thought this was cute, so I would prance around even more on my toe knuckles and repeat the little ditty. I had a great time with all the attention I was getting, but then it was time to head home to Yuma.

Back home at Yuma we went to the train station very often to watch the Indians dance for the people on the train. I often danced with them and I learned three of their dances. Dad was helping to build the High School in Yuma. We used to go to the work site and have a picnic lunch with him. One time when I was three years old I was playing and didn't pay attention to where I sat down. I sat on a cactus and Mom had to pull the needles out of my seat. It was during one of the lunch time picnics that a very large whirlwind came up. Dad was working on the second floor putting up the wall when the whirlwind picked up a large beam which struck him on the head knocking him down. His head was crushed and his neck broken from the impact. I heard some one yell "some bodies hurt." I ran to the building and was the first person to see my Dad. I was not quite old enough to realize every thing. Mom contacted the state of Arizona to make arrangements for the insurance payments she would receive from them. Mom was having a very hard time of it and decided to leave the area. Dad was shipped by freight train to Hot Springs, New Mexico and we rode the passenger car.

Dad was buried where his parents lived as he wanted. While we were there Grandma Euala Jones carved a pull toy truck for me. She was sure good with that knife. I loved to watch her trim her finger nails with it. We took many walks and she talked to me constantly. One walk was to the mineral hot springs where Chief Geronimo and his braves bathed. The one thing I remember her telling me is that my name was Ed and I should not let any one call me Edward or any such thing.

We returned to Mom's parents' home in 1929 and she decided to go back to high school and get her diploma she only had one year to go. She put Georgia Lee in 2nd grade and was able to arrange for me to go to kindergarten even though I wasn't old enough. I was one year younger than the other children. The teacher told my mother that I could color and follow lines with scissors as good as the other children which was a surprise. Mom told every one that she could send me to school dressed in white and I would come home just as clean as when she dropped me off. There was a four foot long fire wood bench with a padded hinged top next to one wall in the corner of the living room. My job was to keep it full and the first person to get up built a fire in the stove.

Mom wanted both Georgia Lee and me to take piano lessons Mom didn't have enough money to pay for both of us so an agreement was made that I could take lessons if I would chop fire wood while Georgia Lee took her lessons. Georgia Lee learned quickly and could even play by ear. I was a little slower learning but after the first year the teacher put on a recital where all her students would play the piece of their choosing. Mom told me how to introduce my piece and bow at the end of my performance. I was the youngest one to perform. When my time came I walked to the front of the stage and announced the name of the piece, went to the piano and for once I played it without making a mistake. When I was through I stood up and bowed really deep almost

9

touching my nose to the floor, I got a standing ovation, Mom cried and I couldn't understand why.

That summer Mom took Georgia Lee and me to Corona, California to visit with a couple of her sisters and a brother. First on the list were Jack and Gertrude Turney and our Cousins Nelda and Winnie Fae. Winnie Fae was a little older so she was put in charge of Georgia Lee, Nelda and me. She took us to a Saturday movie, it was a horror movie. I was the youngest one there and it scared me. I hid my face most of the time and was afraid to watch. That was enough of movies for me and Winnie Fae was scolded for picking that kind of movie.

Gertrude made sure we all had roller skates that would clamp on our shoes. There was a side walk in front of their place where we could skate. We all did pretty good without too many scrapes and bruises and especially with no broken bones. Next to see Uncle Jack and Stella Farnham. They had five children, Jack and Katie were my favorites. Boy did we have fun for a couple of days. Next on the list was Jesse and her two children June and Buzz. Mom and Jessie decided to go to Abilene Texas to a business school. Jessie had no money but Mom was sure that my father's insurance money would be enough to keep us going.

When we arrived in Abilene we found a small apartment that had two bed rooms. Mom would have one bed room and Jessie would have the other one. We children slept on mats in the living room. The first thing to do was for Aunt Jessie and Mom to get registered for the summer. June would take care of us kids. One month the insurance check did not arrive on time. We were out of food and money. One night we had what Mom called, "pine floats" for dinner. That is we had a toothpick and glass of water. I told Mom that I wish we had some peanut butter, and she asked, "What would you do with it." My answer was quit the thing to do as far as I was concerned. I said, "I'd put some on my finger and put it right up there," pointing to the roof of my mouth. My thought was that peanut butter sticks in your mouth and I replied in a muffled voice "it would stick there and I would eventually get full."

One evening there was a dance at the school and Jessie and Mom wanted to go but had no money for the bus and decided to walk. They had read in the paper that there were men grabbing small boys and castrating them. They sold the testicles to local doctors. Mom and Jessie thought it would be safe to walk as there would be two women and four children. No one would bother us. We started walking in late afternoon but soon it started getting dark. Aunt Jessie spotted a car about 1/2 mile behind us that

It would drive a short distance, turn off its lights then a few minutes later would drive a short distance again. This scared all of us so we worked over and under the fence and climbed up in one of the trees so we wouldn't be seen. About this time a large bull appeared so we were afraid to get down out of the tree. After a while the bull left and the car was gone so we continued on our way.

We had to pass what people called a haunted house. Some times the drapes were closed and some times open. The dining room table was also set some times. No one was ever seen in or around the house. We made it to the dance where we kids could sit in chairs and watch except for June as she got to dance a couple of dances. One man took an interest in Mom and gave us all a ride home even though the car only had the front seat and a rumble seat. Boy was it crowded. The next day was Saturday and the man came by the house and asked if Mom, Georgia Lee and I would like to take a ride? Mom got in the front with him, Georgia Lee and I in the rumble seat. He drove us towards the school and pointed out the tame milk cow we thought was a bull, then being macho he drove into the circular driveway of the haunted house, got out and went up to the front door. He knocked on the door and it soon opened squeaking and squeaking all the way. There stood a midget with a riffle in his hands. He asked what we wanted so he explained that he wanted to show us that the house wasn't haunted. They talked and laughed a little while then the man came back to the car and took us home. Mom wanted us to continue with piano lessons. Georgia Lee did not wish to as it was more fun to be with June. I did get a few lessons from a piano teacher that was blind. I listened to him and I am sure I learned much more than the piano.

When the business class was over we returned to California. Mom, Georgia Lee and I went to Porterville. Grandma Farnham tried to teach me how to kill a chicken with an ax. She held a chicken by its legs and placed its neck on the chopping block. With one swift chop the chickens head was off. Now it was my turn. I held the chicken by its legs, placed its neck on the chopping block and with one swift chop I cut its beak off (poor chicken). The next time there were chickens to kill Mom decided she would show both Georgia Lee and me how to wring the chicken's neck. I was first and followed Moms direction and with about three swings the chickens head was in my hand and the chicken was flopping around on the ground. Georgia Lee took her chicken and gave it half a turn and screamed as she let it go, "it's slipping." I didn't realize it at the time but that was her way of getting out of killing chickens. The poor chicken ran around for about ten days with it's head up side down before I could catch it and finish the job. Several years later Georgia admitted that it was her way of getting out of killing the poor chickens.

I spent the summer learning how to milk the cows, feed the chickens, gather the fresh eggs and candle them. We had a well that pumped all the water we needed for the house and one faucet at the back of the house. Grandma used this to water her garden and don't you dare remove the hose. There was no refrigerator but we had a cooler in the shade of the big black walnut tree. The cooler was basically four 2 x 4's about 5 feet long. They had shelves nailed between them to put milk, butter and other food on. The 2 x 4's were covered with burlap material. On top was a water container, the burlap wicked water down and this kept the food cool. I kept the water container full. During the hot summer days Georgia Lee and I would try to swim in the irrigation water when water was in the ditch. Mom tried to keep us in the house during the heat of the day. She taught Georgia Lee and me how to sew with the treadle Singer sewing machine. I caught on real fast and using a flour sack I made a rag doll. Mom painted the face on it. It turned out so good that she suggested I make one for all the neighbor children, so I spent many evenings making dolls for all the kids. I used scrap material from worn out clothes to make the dress and under garments.

Summer was coming to a close and it was time to go to school. Mom enrolled both Georgia Lee me in school. Mom would give us each fifty cents to pay for our lunch for the week. We had to walk about a mile to catch the school bus. I don't know why but all the kids called the bus, "Grasshopper Greens Flying Machine." I had one pair of shoes that I saved for what I called "dress up" so I went to school bear foot. I was younger than the other children in my class. I must have talked a great deal as I was sent to the principles office where she gave me a couple of light swats on my rear end. The principal, Mrs. Bilingsley took a liking to me probably because I was small. This was perhaps the worst punishment I could have received as at recess time she was always out in the yard and she would call to me. Well I knew better than to ignore an adults request so I would go to her. She would pick me up and carry me around the entire recess time. I was so embarrassed in front of the other boys I could have cried. I would some times go to the local candy store and use a nickel of my lunch money to buy candy. This meant that I would miss lunch one day. When Mrs Billingsly saw me out side the cafeteria she would take me in and pay for my lunch. There was one little girl (Betty) that took a liking to me. Georgia Lee was friends with her older sister (Barbara) and

13

often spent the night with her. One Saturday I was allowed to go with Georgia Lee to play. We played hide and go seek most of the afternoon. When it came time to go home Betty asked her mother if I could stay with her that night, she couldn't understand why her mother said no. After all she had a bed big enough for both of us. Her mother explained that I had chores to do at home. It was only 1 mile home so I started walking.

When I got home I had to milk old Betsey and feed the chickens. I poured the milk in the separator and cranked the handle as fast as I could to separate the cream from the milk. The cream and milk were put in separate containers and put out front to be picked up by the creamery Truck. The money from this helped with finances. We saved some of the milk and cream for our own use. Occasionally I would churn butter for our use. In the morning I would collect eggs and take them to the incubator room where I would candle them. I would also weigh them and put them in egg cartons according to size. It seemed there was always chickens to kill and dress out, I always helped with this.

I was allowed to back the Model-A Ford out of the garage and turn it around for mom on Sunday mornings to go to church. One cold winter Friday morning when I got up some one had built a real hot fire in the stove, so hot that the sides of the stove were red. I was sitting on the wood bench with my feet on a foot stool getting ready for school. The foot stool turned over and I fell hitting my left arm and the left side of my face against the hot stove. Mom put lard on my burns then bandaged them. I missed school that day. I was proud as I did not miss any other days.

During the summer there was lots of work to be done, getting the place as nice as Grandpa had it. I know this because Mom kept telling me about how Grandpa had this and how he had that. I wanted to be just as much a man as he and dad had been. Mom helped this by repeatedly telling me to stand up straight like your dad. I would make sure the trash was taken out and burned and I put the cans in a secluded place where visitors would not see them and the place would look cleaner. I didn't know what else to do with them. I would clean the chicken house and I even learned to adjust the mechanical wheel brakes on the Model-A Ford. Mom had me sharpen the ax on grandpas old foot operated grinding stone. All this mechanical stuff filled my mind with ideas that I didn't know how to build. I thought about taking the milk separator apart and using the gears to build something, but I didn't know what.

On the 4th of July there was no money to buy fireworks so Mom took me out and had me set up some old tin cans to use as a target. She had a double barrel 4-10 shotgun and she taught me to use it. I was a pretty good marksman doing as she said. This gave her an idea. The squirrels were always getting in the chicken feeders and the mice in the bag of feed. She said she would give me twenty five cents for every squirrel I killed and five cents for every mouse I killed. It was my job to pay for the shot gun shells and buy extra mouse traps. I just had to bring the tails to show her. In less than a week I had killed so many squirrels and trapped so many mice that she lowered the price to five cents for the squirrels and one cent for the mice. I also killed a couple of rats. They had black and white markings. They were probably some ones pets that had gotten loose. She gave me a nickel for each of them.

Mom enrolled me in second grade and things were going fine until a new boy (Dana Slaughter) came to school. Dana was a bully and picked on every one smaller than him. One day he was bullying me and Betty saw him. Even though she was only in the first grade she ran up and got in between us and said to him, "Go ahead and hit a girl if you know what's good for you." Betty would hold my hand every time she got a chance and parade me around in front of the other girls as if to say, "see I've got a boy friend." Now I had two reasons to run out on the play grounds as fast as I could during recess

15

and lunch periods. I wasn't interested in girls and I didn't want to get picked on.

Mom also started Georgia Lee and me taking piano lessons again. Mom was making enough money to pay the teacher for one of us so she started Georgia Lee with the lessons. She would teach me if once again I chopped fire wood while Georgia Lee took her lesson. Mom looked at me and I nodded my head yes so it was agreed on. Mom was in the orchestra at school and played what she called the Bull Fiddle it was actually a Cello. Why she called it a bull fiddle I don't know. She tried teaching me but the Bull Fiddle was larger than me and I had a hard time trying to hold it up and manipulate the bow at the same time. I did manage to play a couple of simple tunes trying to keep everything standing up right including me.

At school many of us boys were able to purchase a balsa wood glider. We had fun flying them and trying to hit the other gliders. One boy got the idea of putting a pointed nail in the nose of the glider so when you hit another glider it would damage it. Fun trying combat action with them.

Christmas time was difficult for Mom as she couldn't even get a Christmas tree. Grandma got an old broom stick and showed me how to drill holes in it with a hand operated drill. Every one called it an egg beater. I cut some branches off an evergreen tree in the front yard and shaved the end of the branches so they would fit in the holes. We made a pretty good Christmas tree. There were no lights to string on it so we popped corn and threaded a thread through the kernels then hung the strings on the tree. Well at least we had a Christmas tree and a couple of present were put under it. Christmas presents were far and few between. Georgia Lee and Neldafae would get a present one year and I would get clothes. The next year I would get a present and the girls would get clothes. This was my year to get a present. I got a model airplane with a rubber band driven propeller to put together. Some one had given Georgia Lee an older bicycle and sent me an old Flyer Wagon. I proceeded to put the airplane together, although it took me several days as I wanted it to be perfect. While building the plane my mind was absorbing every detail. I began making plans on building a larger one. I had fun flying the plane. I would wind the propeller as tight as I could. I thought if I could get up high the plane would fly further. I climbed up on the roof of the house and launched it and yes it did go further but not due to the propeller, it was a good glider. This worked pretty good but I was scolded for getting on the roof as it could destroy the shingles. I had noticed that some of the shingles were loose and told mom. This meant that the roof had to be replaced. Mom contacted the lumber yard and they came out and measured the roof. The next day a truck came with the roofing material. Luckily for me the instructions were on the packages. Mom couldn't pay to have the roofing put on so it was my job. Those packages of roofing sure were heavy putting them on the roof one at a time was not possible for me so I opened the packages and took the shingles up a few at a time.. I used grandpas roofing hatchet to pound in the nails. I had learned a little about roofing from helping neighbors put a new roof on.

Back at school I was slow running out to the play ground and Dana caught up with me. As he cornered me and started teasing me Betty showed up and told him to leave me alone. Dana looked at her and shoved her out of the way. It made me angry that he would pick on a little girl and I hit him as hard as I could. I hit him in the eye by accident. He ran away holding his eye yelling, "a bee stung me, a bee stung me." Betty wrapped her arms around me and said, "My hero," how embarrassing. She ran around to all the other girls saying that I was a hero. Dana never bothered any one after that. And so the school year ended.

The first day of summer vacation I saw the neighbor in the field next to our place. He was on a tractor cutting hay. I went over to him and asked if I could ride with him. I learned his name was Mr. Cox. After riding with him for about an hour I asked if I could drive. He said sure and changed seats with me. I must have done all right as he offered to hire me to help him on his farm. I explained about the chores I had to do and he said we could probably work around that. The pay was fifty cents for eight hours and that suited me. That evening I told Mom and she agreed to let me work for him if I gave her the money. I continued working for him doing various jobs. Mom often saw me driving his equipment, even his pick up.

On real hot days I would go swimming in the irrigation ditch if it had water in it. What I didn't know is that Mom had contracted to have a swimming pool built in the back yard. At one time a slew ran through the property and some of it was still there. It was in this area where the pool was built. The money I had earned went towards building the pool and it was well worth it as the pool cost $200.00 to build. The pool was 2 1/2 feet deep on one end and 5 feet deep on the other. There was no filter for the water so the pool had to be drained twice a week and wire brushed so moss or algae would not grow. This was a lot of work but at least I could go swimming and cool off when it was real hot.. At the 5 foot end there was a large valve that could be opened to drain the water.

The water flowed several feet away where it made a pond. I noticed that frogs would breed in it. I also remembered that by the river close to town where the water was warm there were a few bull frogs. The first chance I got I headed to the river with a bucket and gunny sack. I caught four bull frogs and put them in the bucket with some water and put the sack over the top so the frogs wouldn't jump out as I walked home. I put the bull frogs in the pond of water from draining the swimming pool. I didn't know if I had male or female frogs but hoped for the best. After a few weeks I saw a cluster of frog eggs in the water. Before the simmer was out I did see some polliwogs but they didn't mature as fast as I expected. Mom told me that bull frogs take about a year to become full grown frogs. I would just have to wait for the frogs to mature so I could butcher them and sell the legs to the local restaurants.

A NEW DAD

Mom invited Clifford Ethan Chilcott (Chili) for dinner one Sunday. I was told to bake a cake while Grandma fixed dinner. This was the first time I met Chili and he seemed like a nice enough person. It wasn't too long before they got married. Mom said she needed help raising the family and thought he would be just fine. We stayed at Porterville with Grandma. Chili built some very long chicken houses and allowed me to help. I spent more time running back and fourth on the rafters than I did helping. Chili made some automatic drinking basins with a way to clean them. Mom ordered a box of Hansen White Leg horn chicks to start what was advertised as superior egg laying hens. We put the chicks in what we called a brooder room in one end of the chicken house. It had a round shaped metal thing about four feet in diameter that was hung so it was only about six inches from the cement floor. There was a place to put an electric light bulb to help keep the baby chicks warm. I watched them grow.

Our cow Betsey had a calf and I grew very fond of it. It was a heifer and I would pet her when ever possible. Mom saw my interest in the calf that I named Fay and saw to it that I joined the Future Farmers of America. Once a month we would have a meeting and learn more about the care and feeding of our animals. Mom helped me enter Fay in the Tulare county Fair and I showed Fay as I had learned and won second prize.

There were four roosters that seemed to grow a little faster than the other chicks. I made pets out of them. As they grew

19

I made harnesses for them from some old leather belts I found. I trained them to pull my wagon. I used a stick with a small bag of seed in it to guide them. They would follow the stick in the direction I pointed. Later in the year there was a parade and Mom couldn't figure out how to advertise our prized chickens. I told Mom I could have the rooster pull the wagon, she wasn't sure but agreed for me to do it. I had the roosters pull the wagon with a small cage on it and a couple of hens in the cage. They pulled the wagon the full length of the parade, it was one mile long and boy, were they tired. Every once in a while I stood on my head on top of the cage. I don't know if it helped sell the eggs and chickens but there sure was a lot of laughing from the on lookers.

We stayed at Porterville the rest of the year. Those long chicken houses gave me an idea. I still had the plans from my airplane kit and decided to build a plane big enough for me to sit in. Every time I had the chance I would go by a lumber yard and pick up some small pieces of scrap wood. I had to buy a few pieces. I saved tin cans so I could make gussets for the major joints. I also picked up rubber inner tubes as they were easy to find. I started putting my plane together following the plans. I laid out all the parts and carried them one at a time to the roof of a chicken house where I could assemble them. I took three wheels off my wagon and put them on for landing and tail wheels. I cut large rubber bands so I could wind up the propeller and it worked but it stopped to quick so I decided to see if I could add propellers to the wings. I took the pedal assembly off Georgia Lee's bicycle so I would be able to wind them up while the main one was still running. I had to figure a way to change the direction of the chain drive. I told mom that I was going to see a friend but instead I went to a junk yard and luckily found a small transfer box. Once I got it working I decided it was time to fly my plane. I got a fence stretcher and using several inner tubes I made a large sling shot. I found a piece of old farm equipment and attached it to the roof of the chicken house and attached a pen to the tail of the plane. I hooked the plane to the sling shot and with one hand pulled the pen and with the other hand released the propeller. The plane took off like a shot and flew about 50 feet before crash landing. Luckily I didn't get hurt. I was able to put the bicycle back together but couldn't straighten the wagon wheels. I hid all the broken plane parts so I could try again later.

Mom gave birth to Nadine Marie in the Porterville Hospital. Chili was not happy living in the country so we moved to El Monte, not far from Los Angeles. He got a job driving a truck delivering milk and other dairy products to grocery stores. We stayed there until the big earthquake hit on March 10, 1933. The school where Georgia Lee and I went was damaged enough that it couldn't be used. When the earth quake hit Georgia Lee was in the bath tub and couldn't get out due to the shaking. I was with a friend of the family in his Model-A Ford. We had stopped at a dairy and he went in to see the people. When the earthquake hit I thought the car was going to drive its self away and I was scared that I couldn't control it. He came running out and asked me if I heard the dishes fall n the house and I told him about the car jumping around so much I thought it was going to drive away. He took me home and let me out then headed for his home to check on his family. There were a couple of families staying with us as they felt their homes were unsafe. There were several after socks and every time one hit every body would run outside to the street and wait for the shaking to stop. I got tired running out side every few minutes so I just stayed put. When things settled down the other families went to check on their homes.

We moved from El Monte to Clearwater where I got my usual bed in the garage. Chili still had his job but was drunk so often he couldn't drive. He would go out Friday night and sometimes would not come home until the next day. It meant that I had to drive the truck and deliver the cases and cans of milk to the different stores. I had to put a couple of pillows behind my back so I could reach the pedals. Mom and I would leave the house around 8:30 in the morning Mom directed me where to turn and which stores to stop at. Once we got everything delivered I would go home and fall asleep. I was always tired as I had to get up and be ready to shag milk bottles on a home delivery milk truck by 3:30 in the morning. This was a seven day a week job. I had a Big Ben alarm clock to wake me up at 3:00 A. M. so I would be ready. I thought the alarm clock with its big bell on top would wake me. Mom always made sure I was awake. The alarm seldom woke me so I got a large bucket and put the clock on top so it would make more noise but that didn't help much as I would just reach over in my sleep and push the alarm button down and go back to sleep. I finally put a nail in the wall and tied a string to the alarm button and the other end to the nail. I had to sit up in bed and untie the string to shut the alarm off. This finally worked so Mom didn't have to wake me any more.

Chili would often go out during the week, have a few drinks and find a lady of the streets. If he couldn't find a street lady he would come to the garage and molest me. He warned me that if I ever told any one he would kick me out of the house. I was afraid to even tell Mom so I didn't act any different than usual. One night I went into the house to go to the bathroom. Chili had arrived a few minutes earlier. As I walked in the house I heard muffled sounds coming from where Georgia Lee slept on a mat and went to see what was going on. I saw Chili half drunk, holding his hand over her mouth and trying to molest her. This was just too much for me to take, I started screaming at him and calling him every name I could think of. Mom heard me scream at him and came to see what was going on. Chili left the room as I described every thing between sobs. Chili came back in the house with a blanket tied up with a rope, he handed it to me and said" I warned you, now get out." I left the house hearing Mom yelling at him. I didn't know where to go so I headed to the park and laid down on a bench. I finally quit sobbing and fell asleep.

CHAPTER TWO

MY FIRST ADVENTURE

I woke up with the first sun rays and tried to figure out what to do. I couldn't go home and had only my blanket. I walked to the boulevard and just kept walking until a truck stopped. The driver asked me why I was out walking so early and where I was going. I just stood there looking at him. He finally said get in boy. I got in the truck and stayed as far away from him as I could. He started asking me questions again and I finally blurted out what had happened. He looked at me in alarm and started driving the truck. He didn't know what to do with me but understood my problem. He stopped at a restaurant and asked me if I would like something to eat. I hadn't thought about food, but yes I was hungry. He also ate breakfast then paid for both of us. We were heading north and soon were driving on highway 99. I became a little more relaxed and soon fell asleep. I woke up when he stopped the truck in a siding by the side of the road. I learned that he had a son about my age and couldn't understand why I was treated in such a way. He pulled out a lunch bucket and shared his lunch with me. After resting a bit he said, "Come on son let's get going and try to figure something out. Our next stop was Weed Patch and he had to pick up a load to take back to Los Angeles.

I started walking and very shortly a car stopped for me. The young man said, "Need a ride?" I said, "Yes, please." I opened the door and got in. He drove for quite a while talking about little things that really didn't matter then stopped by the side of the road. He got out and walked about 20 feet to some brush. He then said, "come over here kid and bring your blanket." This scared me and I got out of the car with my bed roll and ran as hard as I could to get away from him. A car was a little distance away and I ran to the middle of the street and started waiving my arms. The car stopped for me, there was a man and woman in it. Seeing this, the young man got in his car and drove away real fast.

The couple asked me, "What's wrong." I told them about the young man wanting me to bring my blanket and go to him. I was afraid he was going to molest me like my step father had done. They both agreed that I had done the right thing. They asked me all about my getting kicked out of the house and also wondered what my mother had done. I didn't know what mom was doing but I am sure she would give him a piece of her mind. They were going to Tulare and asked if I would like to go that far. I agreed to it. On the way to Tulare I saw a sign pointing to the Tule Indian Reservation and thought perhaps I should go there as I was part Indian. When we stopped in Tulare they bought me dinner and it sure tasted good. I thanked them for the ride and started walking towards the sign but it was getting late so I decided to find a place to sleep.

LEARNING THE INDIAN WAYS

There was a low place beside the road that would give me a little protection I put my blanket down and curled up in it. Sleep did not come very soon as I kept thinking about the last couple of days and wondered about Mom. Would he beat her in a drunken rage or what. I finally went to sleep and when I woke up I continued walking towards the sign. I finally found the sign and headed in the direction it pointed. Finally an old model T Ford pick up stopped and the driver who appeared to be Indian asked, "where you go?" I told him about my being part Cherokee Indian and decided to go to the reservation. He said, "All Indian good I take you there," then asked, "You brave?" My answer of course was that I had never lived as an Indian. When we arrived at the reservation he took me to meet with the chief.

He explained to the chief as much as he could about me then left. The chief told me if I was going to live there I would have to become a brave. This meant I would have to learn how to provide food for a family of two. He then took me into his tepee and we talked about my past and I was told that I would be assigned a brave to help me learn. I spent several days learning to throw a hatchet. I was finally good enough that the Indian brave took me hunting. My first try at killing an animal had me so excited that I missed by a mile. The brave just laughed. When I was finally able to hit my target and kill a rabbit or a squirrel the chief called me over and handed me a small pocket knife and said, "Now you kill bird, bring knife back." Most of the braves had the same kind of pocket knife. I asked about it and found out that several years ago they traded raccoon skins for a box of them. I was again escorted by a brave that led me to where there was lots of brush. As we stood there he put his finger to his lips and motioned me to get down on the ground. He cupped his hand on the ground and put his ear to the knuckles of his hand. We stayed low for several minutes then he signed to me by touching one hand to his fore head then straddling the side of his other hand with his index and middle fingers and last by moving his hands passed each other in front of him. This told me that a white man on a horse went by. He had listened until the man was out of ear shot before standing up and signing to me. He then made a mark on a fallen log and stepped back several feet, threw his knife and hit the target. He showed me how to hold the knife and throw it. I aimed at the target and missed it several times before I even came close. By late afternoon I was getting pretty good at it. We returned to camp and I handed the knife back to the chief.

The brave took me out several more days and each time we would kill something he would take a small flint rock that he carried and show me how to build a fire. He also showed me how to prepare and cook the meat. The medicine man was summoned and he came over to me, said a few words I didn't understand and waved his hands over me. The next day I was again given a knife and a different brave went with me, he wasn't much older than me. He once again showed how to hold the knife to throw it but instead of throwing at the target he led me to a covey of quail, threw his knife and killed one bird. He then motioned for me to kill a bird. We waited until they had settled down and I threw my knife. I killed a bird all right but not the one I was aiming at. He laughed at me and motioned for me to try again. After killing another bird he handed me his flint stone and had me build a fire and cook the birds. My knife throwing got better each day and in about a week I was sent out on my own. The next thing was learning what roots and plants could be eaten. I finally managed to kill enough squirrels or birds and gather enough plants to supply a small family. I also learned how to make pemmican from the dried meat, vegetation and acorns.

One night there was a big celebration (pow wow) with a large fire and dancing. When the dancing and chanting was over the Brave that had taught me the most stopped in front of me and gave me the flint stone he had used to start the fires. The chief motioned for me to come to him, he handed me a knife then took my right arm and made a small cut then did the same to his right arm exchanged blood with me and said, "Now you brave, You Little Chief." Summer was coming to a close and I told the Chief that I should return to the city and go back to school. He said, "School good you come back."

I arrived in southern California after a couple of days and many rides from people that took pity on me and I found the school where I went last year. I looked around for a place to work and live. The park was my home for a few days and I didn't like asking for food. I finally ran into Harry the man that I had shagged bottles for. He asked me what had happened and I told him as best I could. He took me home with him and gave me a hair cut and some jeans that his youngest son had out grown. He let me stay in his garage and furnished my food in exchange for my shagging bottles again. I registered at school and gave Harry's name and address. School was O. K. but nothing seemed to interest me. I thought often about my experience while learning to be a brave. During the first week of school one teacher asked us what we did for the summer. When it was my turn I told about my living on the Indian reservation and finally being able to prove myself as a brave. All the students were interested but the teacher didn't believe me even when I showed her the scar on my arm. She said I just made up the story as an excuse for the scar and that Indians didn't take in small children and teach them how to be an Indian. I quickly learned to watch what I said as she told the principal and other teachers that I didn't tell the truth. This made it very hard to make friends with the other kids as I was now known to be a liar. I finished the year with a C average. I was glad to see the school year end. I was given my report card to take home for my parents to look at and sign. Harry signed for me and asked what I was going to do now. I told him I thought I would try and find my mother. He agreed that it was probably a good idea as he couldn't keep me any longer. The food he was giving me was taking food away from his family. I thanked him for all his kindness, picked up my bed roll and again tried to decide what to do.

As I walked along I noticed a few people looking at me, probably wondering what I was doing with a bed roll. I came to a restraint but didn't go in as I had no money. Instead I went behind and looked for some food that hadn't been eaten. I did find a package of shredded wheat that hadn't been opened. I quickly picked it up then wondered how I was going to eat it; looking around some more I found a clean coffee can and not far away was an old bent spoon in a pile of trash. At least I had a container and spoon. I finally got up enough nerve to go to the front door and asked if there was some work I could do for a small amount of milk. The waitress told me to wait a minute, she left and came back a little later with a small container of milk. She didn't tell me of any work but just pushed me out the door while holding her finger to her lips to keep me quiet. She motioned me to go to the back of the restaurant. She met me out back and gave me a hard boiled egg, kissed me on the forehead waved me goodbye and said good luck. Well at least I had something to eat and decided to go to the Indian reservation.

I stood out on the side walk wondering which way to go. Very shortly a car stopped and the young driver asked me if I wanted a ride. I nodded yes and got in beside him. He said, "You look like you are traveling, where are you going?" I told him about my experience with the Indians and thought I would go back there. He said that he had just been promoted to manager where he worked. The company he worked for was trying to expand and he had just been given an area in Tulare County, $25.00 and the car to get him started. He was heading for Terra Bella just north of Bakersfield. He would like some one to keep him company as he drove all that way and wanted to know if I would care to ride with him. Not really knowing where to go I agreed to ride with him. It took about 2 days to get to Terra Bella. He had bought us several meals. At night he pulled out a sleeping bag and I got my bed roll out. We slept for a few hours then he woke me up telling me that he was hungry and we should get going. We finally found a place to eat in the area called Grape Vine. He was very proud of his promotion and told me all about it and I told him of my Indian experience. We had a great time talking. When we arrived in Terra Bella and said goodbye and good luck I headed in the direction I thought was to the Indian reservation. There were no cars on the road. I did see a farmer on his tractor heading towards his field.

29

THE FRIENDLY BEAR

Eventually a logging truck came down the road, stopped and offered me a ride. He was heading to a logging mill in the mountains and I thought perhaps I could find the reservation from there as I thought it couldn't be that far from the lumber mill. About four hours later we arrived at the mill I thanked him for the ride and started walking. I walked for quite a while in the direction I thought I should go and was getting very hungry. I looked around for some birds or a squirrel and eventually saw a chip monk. It was easy enough to kill by throwing my knife so I dressed it out, built a fire and roasted it. It was pretty good tasting. I was getting very thirsty and started looking for a small stream to get some water. By now I was a long way from the logging mill so it didn't make good sense to go back. Late in the afternoon I decided to find a place to sleep and maybe I could find a stream in the morning. I eventually bedded down under some brush and went to sleep very quickly. In the morning I started walking again and very shortly came to a stream that had trout swimming around in it. I got myself something to drink and very easily scooped out a trout, cleaned and cooked it. Looked like I was going to eat all right.

After another day of walking I decided that I was not going to find the reservation so I looked for a place I could call home for a few days. Looking around behind brush I found the opening to a cave. I looked inside and saw that there was an opening at the other end. This opening looked out over a cliff so there was only one way to get in and there would be fresh air. I put my bed roll down and headed out to find more food. After eating another trout I went back to the cave and even though it was early I went to bed. I was almost asleep when something was bumping my arm. I looked up and there was a large bear. I stayed very still as though I was dead. The bear eventually went further back in the cave and laid down. In the morning it bumped me again with its front paw. Again I made out like I was dead. The bear didn't bother me

30

during the day so I figured I was save enough. The third morning when the bear came to me I very slowly raised my hand and was able to scratch behind its ear. This went on for several days before the bear bumped me very hard and as I sat up it looked at me as if to say, "Come on sleepy head." I got up very quickly and the bear got behind me and started nudging me towards the opening of the cave. I walked outside and went in the direction the bear wanted me to go. It directed me to a berry patch and started eating berries. I tried some and they were good. After this the bear took me every day to either a berry patch or to the small stream where it would reach down and scoop out a fish and push it in my direction. I would pick it up and take it back to where I would build my fire. This went on all summer with the bear taking me to where I could find food and me scratching its back or putting my arm around its neck. I guess the bear adopted me. All in all it was a pleasant experience.

At the first showing of fall I started following the stream down to the valley below. I was sad to leave the bear and I often wondered what it thought about me. As I was walking I came to a large out cropping of rock and started around them when I saw just a few feet away a bob cat. I stopped for a few minutes then backed off, skirted around the rocks and headed on down hill always looking behind me until I was quite a ways away from the bob cat. I finally made it back to the road and civilization where I could start my trip back to Southern California.

I walked along the road until a farmer in his pick up truck came along. He offered me a ride to town then asked me what I was doing out there. I told him about my getting kicked out of the house and was trying to just get along until I could get a job. He asked where any of my relatives lived and I told him I only knew of relatives living in New Mexico and Texas but my dad was killed in Yuma. He suggested that I try and remember the towns where relatives lived and go there and search for any information about my Mother. He let me off on Highway 66, the main road heading south. I had made some pemmican while in the mountains and took out a piece to eat. Sure tasted good, the fish and berry mix worked out great. I finally got a ride in a truck and had to again explain why I was hitch hiking. The truck driver also suggested that I look for my mother. When we got to highway 99 he told that this was as far as he was going and let me out wishing me luck in finding my mother. There were more trucks on the highway than cars and it was hard for them to stop.

A car finally stopped and asked where I was going. They were a young couple with a baby wrapped in a blanket on the back seat I told them I was going to Southern California to go back to school. The baby started to cry and I picked it up. The lady looked like she was worried until she saw me rocking the baby back and forth. I felt good when the baby reached up and started feeling my face. I must have had a big smile on my face as the lady said, "It looks like you enjoy that." I replied, "Yes, I used to have fun watching my younger sister" The lady then asked where my mother and sister were. I explained as best I could what had happened and that I didn't know where Mom and my sisters were. She asked where I thought my mother might be? I really had no idea as I explained that we had friends in Arizona and relatives in New Mexico and Texas. We talked about where I might look for the rest of the trip to Los Angeles. They let me out in down town Los Angeles and I had a hard time finding my way out of town as it was dark and I didn't know anything about the town. I eventually found a place where I would be out of sight and go to sleep. In the morning when I woke up I saw that I was in the door way of a thrift store. When some one finally showed up I asked how to get out of town heading south and low and behold I was on the right street headed in the right direction. I still had some pemmican left so I ate some of it and it still tasted pretty good. I didn't eat a lot of it even though I was hungry as I wanted to save some until I found another source of food.

I saw a delivery truck that had BELFLOWER DELIVERY on the side of it. I waved my arms frantically and the driver stopped. He asked me what kind of trouble I was in as I was wanting a ride so bad. I explained that I was headed for Bellflower so I could go to school and that I had spent all summer in the mountains. I didn't talk too much about it, just that I had lived mostly on fish and berries and made some pemmican. He asked me if he could taste the pemmican so I gave him a piece. He was impressed with the good flavor and had me explain how I had learned to make it. Once again I didn't expect to be believed but he listened to every word and then asked if I would like to go home with him as he lived in Bellflower and tell his family about my living with the Indians? His family was nice and seemed interested in what I had to say. His two girls and one boy were all very young and they seemed easy to be around. Helen his wife asked where I was going to stay and if I was going to go to school. I told her that I had no place to stay and yes I wanted to go to school and church. I showed her my report card from the last year so she would know that I did go to school She motioned to her husband Rupert to follow her. They stepped outside and talked a little while then came back in and offered me to stay with them if I would help Rupert in the evenings and on Saturdays. I was more than glad to accept the offer. I would be required to help him clean his truck and then help load it for the next day. I could go to the same school I attended last year. They would sign for me and I would have a place to live and food to eat. Rupert took me outside and gave me a haircut then showed me the bath room with a bath tub in it and suggested that I get cleaned up. I was so pleased that after I was cleaned up I went up to Helen and told her that she reminded me of my mother. School was still a week away so I had time to get acquainted with the children and the neighbors. Boy this was living. I helped both Rupert and Helen all I could and they were surprised that I was so willing to help. School was nothing to get excited about but I managed to get pretty good grades. The work helping Rupert was not hard and I had plenty of time for my studies and to play with the children. Little by little I told them my complete story. They were sorry for me but at the same time interested in my experiences. I even had to show them the scar on my arm. Helen always had my clothes washed and ironed. One day I asked her to show me how to iron my shirts. As she was showing me she pointed out to me how ragged they were getting and suggested that if I wash dishes for her she would get me some new shirts. Ironing the old shirts was safe enough as I now had some new ones. As I learned to iron I noticed that it was quite heavy. By the end of the school year I was getting pretty good at helping with the house work. They had told me often enough that they wished they knew where my mother was. They were not surprised when I told them that I was going to spend the summer looking for Mom and that I would probably be gone most of the summer. They showed me a map of the United States and pointed out the places where I might look. When the time came for me to leave it was very sad but I knew I had to go. I said goodbye and picked up my bed roll. I turned back and saw her brushing tears away which caused me to do the same thing. I felt like they were a second family to me.

The walk out to the highway was a very lonely walk. It was almost as bad as when Chili kicked me out. I just didn't really know which way to go I decided to go and look in New Mexico as I had relatives living there so I headed for San Bernardino and the freight yards I had heard about.

CHAPTER THREE

LOOKING FOR MOM

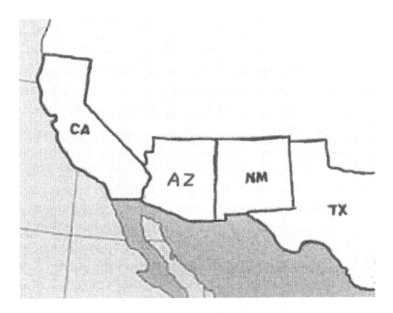

Map of my travel

The map shows the area I traveled while searching for my
Mother and looking for some kind of work. I spent the
winter months in the greater Los Angeles area where I could
go to school and perhaps find some kind of work. I would
hitch hike from there to the San Bernardino area where the
freight trains were assembled for their trip to different parts
of the United States. Arizona, New Mexico and Texas were
the states I wanted to travel in. My travels by freight train
depended on where the train was headed. I knew that people

would look at me when I was asking question about my mother or trying to get work so whenever I would be near a river or lake I would find a secluded place and at least wash my self with water, and some times I would also wash my clothes, put them on wet and continue on my way.

The first train I got on was headed for Tucson. In Arizona I found that work was scarce to nonexistent. There wasn't a lot of things that would attract me except there were a lot of dead animal bones in it due to the lack of rain and the Cattle owners could not afford to feed them. I did earn a small meal once in a while by chopping fire wood. I even tried to hire on at a cattle ranch but was refused as I was so young and would not be able to earn my wages. I told them I was a good worker but that didn't change things as they had no money to pay me any way.

Using the skills I had learned on the Indian Reservation I could kill a rabbit, dove or rattle snake. This would at least keep me from starving. I did not carry a hatchet as this would make me look like I might harm some one. Rattle snake tastes pretty much like chicken except it has a lot of bones in it even more than chicken breast. I often wondered how a snake could wiggle around like it does with such a bony back. A few times when I asked I was allowed to sleep in a barn. This was especially good as while sleeping in the loft, before going to sleep I could see pigeons roosting in the rafters. Next morning as soon as the sun came up I would get up very quietly and stalk the pigeons and could usually capture one or two. These made for a fine meal.

One time when I was hopping a freight train in Barstow I got on the train when it first started moving. I saw two boys about my age running to catch the train but the train had already start picking up speed. (In a freight train yard the tracks are close together and as trains pick up speed they sway back and forth). As the boys reached the car I was in I reached out for the first one, he grabbed the car hand rail and reached for my hand but missed as the train lurched from side to side. He was drug off and collided with the other boy. Both boys were drug under the wheels of the moving train. I never did find out what happened to them. I rode this train all the way to El Paso Texas, hiding each time the train stopped at a station. In El Paso I found that lots of people were looking for jobs, just like every place else I had been. I thought that in the cattle country I could find some kind of job even if it was just feeding the pigs and chickens but like all the other places the people couldn't afford to feed me let alone pay me. While there I traveled around as much as I could. I knew that some distant relatives lived in Texas and thought perhaps I could find one of them. I "by mistake" found myself in Old Mexico and couldn't understand what was being said. I learned from the Indians that when a person is walking in a strange place they should look back to where they had come from every once in a while so they would recognize the area from both directions and could find their way back to where they had come from. I returned to Texas retracing the route I had taken. It was nice getting back to where I could read the signs and understand people.

The days were warm but the nights were very cold, almost freezing. My one small blanket was not enough to keep me warm but it was better than nothing. If I was in town could usually find a news paper that had been left or blown there. If I put the news paper over my blanket it would help as the paper would not only stop the breeze from penetration my blanket but it also worked as kind of an insulator and keep me a little warmer. I had little time to feel sorry for myself as I was always looking for a way to earn food or just plain find something I could eat. One time while in the plains I found an ant hill with large black ants and I was very hungry. I remembered eating grubs I found in rotting logs while in the mountains so I decided to try the ants. I first boiled some then roasted them over a small fire. I tasted one and immediately spit it out even though I was hungry. The ant had a bitter taste and something else I didn't recognize, so much for a little lunch. I threw the rest away. I noticed that the live ants quickly picked up the dead ones and drug them to their nest. Along the way back to the freight yards I saw a tarantula and a couple of scorpions. I never tried them and wasn't about to after my experience with the ants.

LITTLE OLD LADY

While walking to the freight yards I saw a little old lady all stooped over and having a hard time with her balance. She was trying to chop wood. She lived in a ragged old tent and it appeared she was living by herself. I felt sorry for her and as I approached her she looked scared and held the ax up to protect her self. I told her that I had no plans to hurt any one. I finally convinced her that I was O. K. then I suggested that I chop some wood for her and she quickly explained that she had no way of paying me. I said, "That's O. K. I just want to help." The wood she had was scraps of broken lumber from around the train tracks. Her ax was quite old and so dull it wouldn't cut hot butter. I asked her if she had a file and she replied, "yes but it is an old one and not very good." I told her to get it for me and she went into her tent and returned with a file that had many chips broken out of it, but I was able to sharpen the ax to where it would at least cut the wood, still wasn't very sharp though. After I had cut enough wood to last her a few days, she emerged from the tent carrying a couple of biscuits that had been around for a while in one hand and an old stick she used as a cane in the other hand. She offered me a biscuit and said that was all she had but was glad to share with me for the work I had done. I asked her to wait a few minuets as I had to go back in he trees to relieve myself. There was not even an out house close by. I took off and went behind the trees where I was very careful and started looking around. I soon spotted a rabbit and very slowly snuck up on it. I was able to hit it with my knife and kill it. I looked further but found nothing more. Once again I was thankful for what the Indians had taught me about sneaking up on animals, birds etc. I took the rabbit back and skinned it. The lady was very excited about seeing food, so excited she could almost stand up straight. She went to a nearby hole she had dug. She had learned how to catch the dew from the night in an old rusty bucket placed in the hole and rigged up some branches so they would catch the dew and direct it to the bucket. She retrieved enough water to boil the rabbit. As we sat and talked she explained that she and her husband were living on a small ranch they were buying. They stayed until no one could buy eggs or milk from them so they had no money. They exchanged eggs and milk for clothes and other food. Finally they had no money to pay the bank for their property and were notified that the bank would foreclose and evict them. After reading the notice her husband went outside, looked around at their property they had worked so hard to buy and dropped dead from a heart attack. Their two daughters could not help them as they and their families did not live close by and were struggling to make ends meet also. The lady asked me to stay the night as it would be warmer in the tent than out on the ground some place. I told her that I thought I should be on my way. She asked me, "Where that would be?" I told her that I really didn't know but I remembered that my Great Grand Mother had by chance named the town of Silverton, Texas. I said, "That is where I am going to try and find relatives."

It was still early in the afternoon so I didn't go to the freight yards. I searched around for some kind of food that I could get for the lady and myself. I found no edible vegetation but I did find a snake that was sunning itself. I was able to kill it with a rock, skinned it and took it back to the lady and she was delighted to see a little more meat. She again asked me to spend the night but I refused as I wanted to be on my way.

I headed for the freight yards and seeing no one I ventured to the train depot. There was only a clerk present and he immediately informed me that I could not stay the night in the depot. He also warned me against hopping a freight car. I tried to look as innocent as I could. I ignored his comments and asked him if one of the trains might be going towards Silverton. he replied, "the town was fairly new and no trains stopped there" pointing to the north west. I figured that was the direction I should go. He said, "There were no trains scheduled to go in that direction for a couple of days as business had dropped off a great deal the last couple of years." The depression affected every thing.

A little later I saw a train ready to leave heading west. Not wanting to stay in the area I hopped one of the freight cars that had a few sacks of grain stacked in one end. These made a perfect hiding place. I suspect the sacks were placed at one end by those loading the freight car knowing they would make a warm hiding place for some one. There were already a couple of men in the car and when they saw me they made a place for me. Every time the train stopped at or left a depot they would hide but keep an eye out for any new comers or Bulls. I at long last had a few hours of warm sleep. The train stopped in Tucson, Arizona and the men warned me to be on the look out for Bulls as they were very hard on those riding freight cars. We all jumped off before the train came to a complete stop and headed for a bunch of trees a short distance away. When we decided we were well hidden the men asked me to join them and four other men for dinner. I explained that I had nothing to offer. The men dug into their packs and cans of food and scraps began to appear. There was a mixture of beans, fish, vegetables and other assorted food which was placed in one pot and heated up. We all took out our utensils for eating and they laughed at my old tin can and bent spoon. Ah! The hobo stew tasted great. We had a great time telling where we had been and what we had done. When I explained about my experience with the old lady they were pleased at what I had done but sorry for the lady. One man asked me what she looked like and I explained every thing I could think of. He kept asking me questions about what she looked like and where I had seen her. This man was very interested in finding her. I explained her location in as much detail as I could then asked, "Why are you so interested?" He explained that he though the lady might be his Mother in law. Even though he had not found work he and his wife decided that he should try and find her. They decide he should look in the vicinity of where the farm was. He had already been searching about two months with no success and had almost given up. He had never thought about looking around the railroad tracks or train depot. My description gave him hope and he left in search for her on the next train headed in the direction I came from.

The next day there seemed to be very little train traffic so I decided to ride on my thumb. I found my way to the nearest road, couldn't tell if it was a highway though. It did appear to be a little more heavily traveled so it must by the highway. Some times it was hard to tell the main highway from the secondary ones. Route 66 had not been completely finished and the government had little money to spend on it. An old pickup truck finally came along and stopped for me. I asked the man if this was the highway to Arizona and he replied, "yes and he could take me to the next town which was Lordsburg, New Mexico and that I should stay on the highway as it would take me to Phoenix, Arizona." He reached in a sack and pulled out a peanut butter and jelly sandwich looked me straight in the eye and said, "Are you hungry?" My answer was, "Yes starving." GOOD!

In Lordsburg I planned to spend the cold night by the side of the road in a ditch so the wind wouldn't bother me and I would be a little warmer. About 10:00 P. M. a police car pulled up and a police man got out, came over to me and asked who I was and where I came from. I gave him my name and said I was from where ever I could find work and food. He told me to get in the car so I did all the while wondering what I was in for. At least it was warmer than the ditch. We went to the police station which also housed the jail. The policeman told me to go into the building. I walked in and was greeted by the desk sergeant. I was instructed to empty my pockets and put my things in a paper bag that he gave me. I was then told to go in to the jail where another policeman was holding the door open for me. As I went in I was told to take my clothes off, handed a towel through the pass through opening. The officer pointed down the hall and said for me to take a shower. When I got through with the shower I was told to put my clothes back on. I was called back to the pass through opening and handed a great big cheese burger, fries and a glass of milk. I was given plenty of time to eat then handed a couple of sheets and a blanket. The officer pointed towards a group of bunks and informed me that I should sleep. I was asleep in about half a minute, a comfortable bed and warm blanket did it's duty. I slept all night and woke up about 8 A. M. I was told to get dressed and was surprised to find my clothes clean. Before I was released I was handed a plate with a couple of eggs, 2 strips of bacon and some toast with jam on it. To be treated like this I could have stayed in jail forever. The door was opened so I could leave and I was handed the bag with my belongings in it. The clerk told me to check and make sure all my things were there. I was ready to leave but was stopped and asked if I wanted my bed roll too. Of course I answered yes as I need my bed roll for the nights ahead of me. I was again told to check to make sure everything was there. There was a new blanket in place of my thread bare one. My old rusty can had been replaced by a new one, but I still had my old bent spoon. The policemen then took me back to the place where they found me. I was handed $5.00. They had taken up a collection for me. I thanked them and watched them drive away.

I stood by the side of the road long enough to wonder if I wouldn't be better off going to the freight yards and finding a freight train going in the direction I wanted to go. Mid afternoon a model T Ford stopped for me. The elderly man told me he was going to Globe, Arizona and could take me that far if I wanted. I said, "that would be great." Heading west we saw lots of interesting things. I remember traveling through the Navajo Reservation and seeing things like the Hogans that the Indians lived in. These were fairly large mud huts. They were about 6 inches thick and the mud on the outside was applied like plaster. The huts were thick to keep the hot sun out in the summer and hold the heat in the winter. There was a fire pit in the center for cooking food and heating in the winter and cold mornings. There was a hole in the top to let the smoke out

Hogan

The Indians would gather wood and grub for roots where ever they could find it. The man told me that when the Indians killed an animal the meat was cooked, cut in small pieces and pulverized with vegetables, and cooked again this made what they called pemmican. A hole was dug in the ground and lined with the largest leaves they could find. A layer of pemmican was placed in the bottom of the hole on the leaves and covered with leaves or vegetation and another layer of pemmican was placed on top of that and again covered with vegetation. This continued until all the pemmican was used or the hole was full. A layer of vegetation was placed on top then covered with dirt and a large rock put on top to keep animals out. so I learned a little more about making pemmican.

As we drove along I saw some large Saguro cacti. I asked about it and the man stopped right there in the road, got out and very carefully cut out a large piece of it and brought it back. He gave me a small piece to chew on and it was very wet. he explained that while in the plains like this when you got thirsty you could always chew on a piece of Saguro to quince your thirst. In wet areas where there was a small lake and damp enough that prairie grass would grow you would occasionally see a Lesser Prairie Chicken.

Prairie Chicken

The man then showed me which levers to move while he cranked the motor. We proceeded on to Globe where he let me out, wished me good luck and drove off.

In the early afternoon a big fancy, powerful looking limousine stopped for me. I didn't know if I should get in but the large well dressed man motioned me in. I had no longer gotten seated than the man told me to look in the glove box. When I opened it I was scared as there were two pistols in side. I was told to close it and look in the back seat. There was glass between the front and rear seats. When I looked in the back I wondered what kind of trouble I had gotten into as there was a submachine gun there. The man evidently saw the look on my face as he then reached inside of his coat and showed me a badge. He informed me that he was an F B I agent and was transporting his car to California. As we drove along he explained to me that the F. B. I. usually shipped their cars by rail, but this time it was recommended that he drive. He never did explain the reason for all the guns. As we drove along he did tell a little more about transporting his car. There were several different agents driving on different highways and roads checking to see how many young people were out on their own. We drove for about 3 hours. The man telling me the different F. B. I. assignments he had been on. One that caught my interest was when he was on a task force that was working on one of the gangster groups. He couldn't tell me which one, but it was very exciting to my young mind when they finally caught up with the gangsters and after a brief gun battle they caught the gangster mob and there was only one fatality. I felt like I was in with a really important person and I would be able to tell this story to all I met. As we were still a long way from his destination he decided to stop at the next town he decided that he should stop for the night. My heart sank as I was afraid I would never see this important man again. The town was Phoenix. He pulled into a service station, told me to stay put. he got out and talked to an attendant for a few minutes. The attendant pointed in the direction we were going so the man came back and we drove a short distance to another service station. When we arrived at the next service station he got out and talked to the attendant who pointed to a two story building next door. The man came over to me and said that I should go to that two story building. He handed me 25 cents and said that the building was called a flop house and for the 25 cents I could get a bed for the night. He also said that when I got up I should come back to the service station and ask if that gent man had left yet. If he had not left I was to wait for him. So I went to the building, knocked on the door and I heard a lady say come on in son. Gent man is the way he pronounced gentleman with his New York accent.

The attendant at the 1st station had informed the lady at the flop house that I would be coming. The lady was very nice; she gave me a glass of milk and took me up stairs where there were several cots. She pointed to one and said that was where I was to sleep for the night. She took my 25 cents and said that there would probably be two or three more people come up to bed that night. She said she would tell them that I was there so they should be quiet. Here again I felt the comfort of a warm bed. I slept through the night and got up feeling refreshed. I got up about 6:30 A. M., dressed and went down stairs. The lady met me with a piece of hot home made bread that she had buttered and a glass of milk. Now I really felt that the F. B. I. agent was special due to all the attention I was getting just for having been with him for a few hours. I went to the station, asked if the gent man had left yet and was informed that he was still there. He was across the street at a small restaurant having breakfast. The man came over very shortly after that, greeted me as son and told me to get in the car. We drove for a couple more hours, all the time he was thrilling me with his stories and when we were in the dessert area he pointed out low areas by the side of the road.

He explained that when there had been a heavy rain in the dessert and the water that collected in the low areas lasted for several days a person could stop and look in the water. There they could see prehistoric frogs. These frogs would be very small. The frogs would hatch out when they had been wet a couple of days, emerge from the mud. They would mature in about 3 days, mate and lay eggs in the mud. They would survive until the water dried out and they would die. A few years later when it would rain hard enough for the water to stand for several days the eggs would hatch out. Boy was I getting an education. We arrived at Desert Hot Springs in the California dessert and he told me that he could take me no further. He took me to a restaurant, bought me breakfast, shook my hand and said goodbye and good luck.

I finally got a ride from a long distance truck driver heading for Los Angeles. The man only had a couple of peanut butter and jelly sandwiches and shared them with me. He drove through the night stopping very little and we arrived in L. A. about mid morning. I had shared some of the stories the F. B. I. man had told me and he wondered if perhaps some of them were made up. That idea didn't set well with me as I believed all the stories. I thanked the man for the ride and left.

I knew it was getting close to time for school to start so I headed to the town of Clearwater where I had shagged milk bottles with the hope that the dairy could find something for me to do. As it turned out it took me a couple of days to go the few miles getting short rides of a mile or two at a time. I finally located the dairy and was greeted by the owner. Seeing my bed role he asked me where I was staying and I answered, "No particular place." After talking to him for a while he said that I should come back the next day. I went into the town and used what little money I had left to get something to eat and rent a room. I thought I would have a better chance of working at the dairy if I were clean.

When I arrived at the dairy about noon the man came out to greet me with a big smile on his face. He told me that I could stay there as they had a small building out back that had a bunk, shower and small bath room if I could wash bottles every night from 8 P. M. to midnight. He also said I could have all the dairy products I wanted, but they had no money

47

to pay me. I felt like this was a great deal so I agreed to his offer. He showed me the large sinks with the revolving brushes and said he would get me started that night. So I took my bed roll to the small building, fell over on the bed and slept for a couple of hours, got up and went to the milk house where I drank a quart of milk. I met the man at about 7:30 and he proceeded to show me how to wash the bottles. He watched me until he knew I could do the job. He then told me to place the clean bottles in a milk crate, stack the crates 3 high and wheel them into what he called a steam room. This room was about 20 feet square and lined with metal sheets. When I finished with all the bottles I was to close the steel door and go over and turn on a certain switch marked boiler. This would start the boiler working and would fill the room with steam for about an hour. This sterilized the bottles. I finished washing bottles that night and boy was I tired. It took me longer than 4 hours but I thought I might get faster as I learned how to arrange everything and speed up the way I washed the bottles. I went to the little building and stepped inside and to my delight there was a switch to turn on a light. It was a bare bulb hanging down from the ceiling on an electrical cord. I laid down on the cot and didn't even remember covering my self up.

When I woke up it was already mid morning and I still had to find work and check up on school. I drank a pint of milk and started walking to town. It seemed like I walked a very long distance but I knew it was only a few miles. I stood around on the main corner for about 30 minutes wondering what to do and which way the school was when I saw a man coming towards me with a bunch of news papers under his arm. I wondered what he was doing with so many news papers and decided to ask him. He told me that he could earn a little money by selling them to people walking by and also to some people in cars as they stopped at the stop sign. I told him about my looking for a job and perhaps he knew where I might look. He let me know very loudly that if he knew where to get a job he wouldn't be selling news papers on the street corner for a few pennies a day. I walked away from him not wanting to be yelled at. I walked about half a mile and saw a small truck parked by the side walk with a bunch of news papers stacked in the back. There was a man sitting in the truck. Remembering the man selling papers I thought that perhaps I could earn enough money to buy some food. so I went up to the man and asked if it would be possible for me to sell papers on a street corner. He said, "I can't tell you if it is right now but come back here tomorrow and I will tell you if my boss said it's all right." That sounded like it was a put off, but I did need some money so I asked what time and he said that 10 A. M. would be fine. I then asked if he knew where the nearest Junior High School was and he pointed North. He said it would be a couple of miles. I don't know why I was so intent on going to school, I just knew that it was required and I didn't want to get in trouble. I headed towards the school and when I located it I was too late to register as the school was closed for the day.

I was hungry and decided to return to the dairy where I could at least have some milk. It was late afternoon when I arrived. I went into my room and found a couple of slices of bread with a little jam on them on a dish. So after another pint of milk and my bread and jam sandwich I washed the dish and headed into the building where I was to start washing the bottles. By the clock on the wall I saw it was only 7:30 but thought if I started early I could be finished by 11 P, M, There was a radio playing in that room, I believe it was always on. I listened to the news which to me was very sad. One man shot another in a fight over a job and many men trying to get a job at the local foundry etc. Then the world news came on and I heard them talking about the New Deal that President Roosevelt had started and would make several jobs for the men and women of the country. Then there was a music program. A few of the songs I had heard before like, "Brother Can You Spare a dime" This was sung by Bing Crosby but one song caught my attention. This one I believe

49

was written for the young people that were roaming the streets: "Small Fry strutting by the pool room. Small Fry should be in the school room. Small Fry put down that cigarette you ain't a grown up high and mighty yet. Oh me oh my small fry. Small fry dancing for a penny." This struck me in the right place and I knew I had to find my way back to school. I remember how nice it was to hear music for several hours. I always loved music and this gave me a kind of rhythm to wash the bottles by. When I finished I returned to my room, took a shower and headed for bed.

I must have fallen asleep immediately as the next thing I knew it was day light. I drank some milk and headed for town. I went to the school and tried to register. I was informed that I had to have my last years report card, an address and the signature of my parent or guardian. This posed a problem as no one was my guardian and I didn't know where my mother was. I went back to where I saw the man in the truck and sure enough he was there. I went up to him and he said that I could sell papers and he would show me which corner. The newspapers were $0.05 each. For every ten papers I sold I would receive $0.05. He also told me that I could sell papers in either Clearwater or Hines if I wanted. Clearwater and Hines are two small towns right next to each other. They eventually merged and became known as Paramount. I was sure I could sell more than ten papers. I asked when I should start and he replied, "right now." He said I looked like the kid that was shagging milk bottles in Hines for the Paramount dairy. I told him that I had been shagging milk there but left home when my step dad ordered me out. You must be the kid I am thinking about. He said that my parents were the talk of the neighbor hood for a while, they knew about my drunk step dad and that he had kicked me out. He went on to say that my mother left him at that time taking my sisters with her. The neighbors were so angry with him that he had to leave town because they had threatened him with violence. He asked me where I was staying and I told him I was staying at the Paramount dairy.

He asked how I made out at school and I told him what I needed. He said to ask Mr. Olson at the dairy if he would sign for me. I told him that I always carried my report card for identification if I happened to need it.

I sold about 30 papers that day so I at least made $0.15, enough to buy a bowl of chili and a cold drink with $0.07 left over. I went to a small restaurant in Clearwater and had the chili and a soda. I returned to the dairy and found Mr. Olson. He said that he would sign for me if I promised to not get into any trouble. I of course told him that I would stay out of trouble to the best of my ability. He signed the paper for me and I thanked him for it. This meant that I could return to school the next day and register. I took my turn at washing bottles that night and went to bed very tired. The next morning I headed for the school after selling a few papers and upon arriving found I was the only one registering that early in the day. I was able to choose some of the programs I thought I would like. I first chose drama, choir and then art. What else would a kid choose? There were classes I had to take besides those three. Then I presented them with the paper Mr. Olson had signed, showed them my last years report card and I was enrolled in school.

I returned to town and picked up the papers I would sell. I sold 35 papers in Clearwater and then took a hand full to Hines where I sold another 10 papers. This meant that I had earned enough money so I could afford to get a haircut which cost $0.25. I told the barber that I wanted an adult haircut and wanted a little of the side burns left on. The barber did a nice job just like I wanted and I paid him the two bits. Mr. William's told me how nice I looked and that it would make it easier for me to sell papers. He was right I did sell more papers and after a few days I began to have regular customers which meant I had a good idea of how many papers I would sell. I continued selling papers for about two months when the man I now know as Mr. William's said that a morning paper route was opening up if I could get a

51

bicycle. He also stated that the reason he was offering it to me is that I always showed up at the correct time and he liked that. When I finished selling papers that day I had my usual bowl of chili and a soda. I went back to the dairy and told Mr. Olson about the offer, but I didn't have enough money to buy the bicycle. He asked me how I would be able to get up at four A. M. and I told him I had spent all my money that day to buy a Big Ben alarm clock to wake me up. He left after saying he would be back in about thirty minutes. When he returned he handed me $2.50 for the down payment and told me where to find the bicycle store.

I got up early the next morning as I had lots to do, drank my usual pint of milk and headed out the door. I found the bicycle shop, went inside and saw what I thought were the neatest bikes I had ever seen. The owner of the shop asked me what I wanted and I said I was hoping to maybe get a bicycle. He asked me if Mr. Olson had spoken to me about his shop so I told him about Mr. Olson handing me the money. I looked around for a little while and saw this neat blue bicycle with a head light and horn. The price tag hanging on it had in big bold letters, "special only $27.00" I told the man I liked that one but couldn't afford it. He told me if I had $2.50 I could make a down payment and then pay him $1.00 every week. I reached out my hand and said very loudly DEAL! I told him that it needed a rack over the back fender and he pointed to several that were hanging on the wall. I chose the strongest one and asked how much. #2.00 and it would be put on for me. I suspect that Mr. Olson had made an agreement with him. I gave the man the $2.50 and signed an agreement paper. The next day I arrived a little early to sell papers and Mr. William's was pleased to see the bicycle. I would have to wait about ten days for the route to open up but should ride along with the other boy that was delivering the papers so I could learn where the customers lived. So getting up about 3:45 A. M. I headed out to meet the other boy. I was so excited that I forgot to drink any milk.

When I met the other boy I immediately liked him. His name was David. He was very patient with me, showed me how to fold the papers, put them in the saddle bag and even bought me a donut about six in the morning. We completed the route so I went to where I sold papers and had another good day. Things were looking up for me. Mr. William's told me that when I started delivering papers on my own I could stop selling papers on the street. I went to the Paramount dairy mid afternoon and took a nap after setting my alarm clock so I could get up in time to drink milk then wash the bottles. Next morning I got up early enough so I wouldn't be late for the paper route. That night I was in good spirits as I washed the bottles. When I had finished I realized that the next day was Sunday and I hadn't been to church in quite a while. I set my alarm clock for 3:45 A. M., drank my milk and headed for town on my new bicycle.

I met David in time to help him fold the papers and put them in the bag. When I was through with the paper route I went to the restaurant and ordered pancakes. I sold a few papers and started looking for a local church. Most churches started about 10 A. M. so I only had a short time to find one. I located a church near by, l looked at the reader board and discovered that I could make it there after selling papers and most important after delivering papers on the route. I went into the Church building and was surprised at the service. Each time the preacher would say something that the people liked, they would jump up, raise their hands and shout hallelujah or something like that. Some times they would roll over on the floor. I didn't like what I saw and left early. I went back to my corner and started selling papers again. Sunday paper was $0.10. In the afternoon when I sold a paper to a well dressed person I would ask where I could find a church. By the time I was through I had several addresses, I also learned that the church I had attended was called a, "Holly Roller Church." I went to the small restaurant and had my usual bowl of chili and a drink.

When Wednesday came I had enough money that I could pay the man at the bicycle shop $1.00. He thanked me and wrote it down in a book. I continued working and learning the paper route until David turned it over to me. The first day of school I arrived all spit and polish and followed my schedule. There was a boy in my drama class that I liked right off the bat. I later saw him in Gym class and learned that his name was Paul. He had been to this school before and invited me to go see the gym coach as he was a nice guy. Paul introduced me to the man and suggested that I should learn some of the regulations. He said there was a punishment if you did something wrong. He went on to explain that if a person sassed the teacher, talked in class when they should not have' or got in a fight were the things that were the most likely to get you in trouble. The coach showed me this big paddle that had several holes in it. I asked what it was about and was informed that If you did something wrong in school you would get between 3 and 10 swats with the paddle. The holes were there to make it sting really bad. The paddle was about 12 inches wide and 16 inches long with a long handle. I did not plan on getting in trouble, especially after seeing the paddle.

Paul and I became good friends and were together as often as I had time. He lived at home and explained that his dad was trying to get a job at the local foundry and his mother ironed clothes for the lady whose husband owned the local hardware store. Business was not very good at the store but they were able to squeak by. The hardware store was one of my customer and I learned that the man purchased the paper to attract men to come in, read the paper look at the help wanted adds and might buy a little something. Most of his customers purchased chicken feed or food for their cows.

Paul and I were the usual clowns in drama class. We liked being together and having fun and the drama teacher was a good sport. One day Paul caught a mouse and thought we should put in the teachers desk but he was afraid he might get in trouble. I took the mouse from him and held on to it for a while. The teacher left the room for a few minutes so I decided to do as Paul had suggested and I put the mouse in the top middle drawer of the teacher's desk. When the teacher came back in the room every one was very quiet. You could see by the way she acted that she suspected something. She began describing to us how marionettes work and asked if we would like to make one. Most of us agreed, so she went to her desk to get a pattern, opened the drawer and the mouse jumped out. She let out a scream then looked straight at me and said, "Catch it." I suppose she called on me because I was probably laughing the hardest or perhaps she somehow knew it was me. I cornered the mouse and caught it by the tail and as I carried it out, I went as close to her as I could without looking too suspicious. When I returned she and the class was laughing. I guess the joke was on me. I liked this class and the teacher. She obviously knew that I was living on my own as she never reported me, so I didn't get in trouble and get a few swats from the paddle.

My next class was Social Studies. The girl sitting in front of me was always disagreeing with the teacher. We talked mostly about the depression and how it affected us and our families. When we had a discussion in class the girl always took the negative side of the subject and I took the positive side. The girl blamed the president for the problems and I took up for the president saying it was not his fault but the stock market failure. I said that she should look at the jobs the president was creating like the W. P. A. I didn't realize how much I had learned from reading the papers I had sold and delivered. Our team became popular in the class.

Then came choir which I dearly loved. We sang all the familiar songs for Easter etc. We were told that we should practice every chance we could get. Memorize tunes and words and if we were good enough we could try out for parts in an operetta to be given at the end of the year. Then it was lunch time I went to the cafeteria and ate lunch. After lunch I went out to the ball field and saw a bunch of boys on the outside edge. They seemed to be gathered in small groups of five or six. I saw Paul in one of the groups so I went over to that group. They were playing marbles. There was a circle drawn in the dirt and several marbles were in the middle. I saw one marble that looked prettier than the others. Paul told me that it was the taw of one of the other boys. The taw is the special marble that a boy uses to try and knock other marbles out of the ring. He had tried to knock marbles out of the ring so he could add them to the others he had in a small cloth sack. His taw had hit a couple of marbles but got stuck in the circle. This meant that if another boy knocked it out they could keep it. The players would place their hand close to the ground with the palm up. The taw was placed on the second joint of the middle finger, the index finger was to touch the ground. The thumb was used to shoot the taw hard enough to knock marbles out of the ring. The taw was aimed for a glancing blow against a marble and then continue out of the circle. I watched for a while then went to clean up after lunch.

In Gym class I noticed a boy with one arm who was playing base ball. He could catch and throw the ball as well as the other boys. When it was his turn to bat I wondered how he could hit the ball. Some of the other boys did not want him to bat saying that they could do it better. He told them he wanted to try but the boys thought he couldn't do well and started taunting him saying, "One arm bandit, one arm bandit." This didn't set too well with Paul and me so we took sides with him. He was finally allowed to bat when the coach showed up, and boy could he hit, better than many of the other boys including me. When gym class was over I took a shower and headed for my English class.

After school I spent a couple of hours every day going to the houses where I delivered papers to collect for the paper as people had to save their pennies to pay for it. I had a book with all their names and addresses.

When I was through collecting for the day I went to the Paramount dairy where I could take a nap before washing bottles. I set my alarm clock so I would have time enough to drink some milk and then wash the bottles. Every Wednesday I would go the bicycle shop and pay the man $1.00 from my collections. I recorded this in my school note book so when it came time for me to pay the man for the papers I had delivered I could tell him what I had done. He was very pleased with me and I had a little money left over so I could buy clothes and eat. The first month I purchased a pair of shoes to replace my worn out tennis shoes. I bought a pair of good sturdy black ones. I was very proud of those shoes. I was very careful with my money and had enough for my morning donut and still have money for school lunch.

It was almost my birthday and I felt sad that there was no one to sing happy birthday to me. What I didn't know was that Paul had told the drama teacher about my birthday. Much to my surprise in the drama class there was a cake large enough for every one to have a piece and there were thirteen candles on it. The principal and a couple of other teachers showed up. The teacher led them in singing happy birthday, cut the cake and put the pieces of cake on paper plates and passed then out to every one. There was also a half pint of milk for all of us. She had talked to the school principal about me and a collection was taken from the teachers to purchase the milk. I learned later that she had baked the cake. Boy was I one happy and lucky thirteen year old kid. We learned at this time that we would read a story then write a puppet show from that story. We all had to read a book that we thought would work then make an oral report on it. I didn't have time to pick out and read a book, I knew if I tried to read, I would fall asleep. When it came time to report on the book I had no report but the teacher didn't call on me. We chose a story about a clown act in a circus. We wrote our own story around the book report and all of us went to work making our marionettes, the teacher guiding us all the way. With so many girls in the class it ended up with a love story between a clown and a trapeze acrobat.

The next day the teacher brought in material so we could start making the marionettes. This was a challenge for most of us. The hardest thing for me was making all the joints bend in the right direction. Knees to bend backwards, not in all directions. Arms bent in all directions too. The teacher helped me on that and laughed with me about it. We also got to volunteer for the part we wanted. Well I have always thought of myself as a clown so naturally I selected that part, several other boys including Paul wanted that part also. One part was left untouched, it was the janitor that would clean up after the clown and trapeze acts were complete. Of course no one wanted such a lowly part. It looked like we were going to have to pick a different story and this would make us change our marionettes. We would have less time to practice for our part in the assembly. The teacher looked unhappy and I felt sorry for her, so soft hearted me I said I would take the part. There were only a few of us that were willing to get up in front of a lot of people so many students made their marionettes to look like dolls. The next thing we had to learn was how to work the six strings that made them move. Two strings tied to a straight board about 7 inches long one attached to each hand Four strings to were tied to another piece that looked like a cross. The string on one end of the long piece was attached to the head and the other end was attached to the waist. The two stings on the cross piece were attached to the knees. I had little to do during the time the others were practicing so I went to the back of the room and practiced walking my marionette and making it bend over to pick up things. I made a small broom and tied it to one hand. I found out with a lot of practice I could make it look like the broom handle got between its feet and it would fall. While Paul and the others were perfecting their part I kept learning new things my marionette could do. When it came time for me to join the others in practice I had the janitor walk slowly, bend over and pick up imaginary pieces and put them in a bag attached to the hand with the broom in it. I could make it look like he was sweeping. We went through this a couple of times and the teacher said I did just fine. The next day we had to practice once again but this time I made the janitor appear clumsy. The students laughed at him and the teacher applauded when he crawled off the stage area. It was decided that I should practice this and use it when we gave our presentation.

In the choir our teacher started us learning what our operetta was going to be. There were songs and speeches to memorize. We had the rest of the semester to learn and practice. I had one small solo and the rest of the time I sang with the class. Social Studies continued with debates about what was happening in the world. We were asked to bring in articles we had found in the paper. Many of the students' parents did not take a paper so they did not have a paper they could read. I asked the man I sold papers for if he would give me two or three day old papers to take to school, this was very helpful to those who had no paper to read at home.

Next was art class, we were instructed to draw a picture of an animal we liked best. Paul chose a dog and I chose a horse. I found that I was pretty good at drawing a horse, much to my surprise. The teacher then told us to draw only the head of the animal and I am happy to say she pointed out little things that made our drawings better. When the teacher was satisfied she instructed us to bring in two pennies the next day. Some of the students couldn't bring in any money and Paul was one of them as his father was not working so I gave him the two cents. The teacher helped the other students that had no money, trying all the time not to let any one see her. The two pennies paid for a small piece of leather about the size of a wallet. We soaked the leather in water for a few minutes, then traced our drawing on it with a blunt pencil like tool. The next day a few tools were handed out that would make a permanent impression on the leather. We were instructed to follow the lines that we had traced on the leather with the tool. You had to be careful as the tool was hot. When we were finished with that we were given a very thin piece of leather the same size as the original piece. We had to hold the two pieces together and punch holes about 1/4 inch apart all along the ends and one side, making sure our animal was upright. Next we received what looked like a very thin, long shoe lace. We laced the two pieces together making sure the ends were tucked in very tight. We now had a neat looking wallet. I was excited as I could carry my things in the wallet and not in a paper sack. Then there was Harold who was about a foot taller than me. He could always find me when I was going from one class to another. He was a nice enough person but I didn't like being close to him as his breath smelled like horse manure. He had his good points though. When any one approached me and Harold thought they might pick on me or give me trouble of some kind he was always taking my side. He was big enough that no one dared cross him.

One afternoon while I was out collecting I saw three boys riding their bicycles as fast as they could. As they rounded the corner two of them collided and fell. One boy hit his head on the curb; I went running over to see if I could help. The boy that hit his head had a big cut in his scalp and was bleeding badly. A couple of adults showed up and started to cry. One woman went to her house and got a towel while the other stood by trying to console the boy. They wrapped his head in the towel, brought a car over and helped him in. The next day I asked how the boy was and was informed that he was in the hospital with a concussion. He had to have several stitches in his scalp. The bicycles were O. K. though and that would please the boy as he liked to ride. I am sure he learned to be more careful, but I didn't learn from his experience. I continued to ride my bike backwards while sitting on the handle bar and jumping curbs. Because my paper route and my jumping was so hard on my bike, I took it apart once a week to clean and lubricate it. When I had to buy new tires I would save the old ones and put them over the new one and tape them in place. There was one area where I delivered papers that was nothing but a dirt road and it got real muddy when it rained. It was hard to get traction in the mud so I purchased some very small chains and put them over my rear tire. Didn't do any good though so I wound up pushing my bike through the mud. I had to get new parts for the real axle which was a single speed New Departure. I was very pleased with myself as it took me just three months to pay for the bicycle and repay Mr. Olson the money I owed him. My winter went along great. With the fog, and rain it was cold in the mornings so I went to the Good Will and purchased some jeans and a used leather jacket for a grand total of $1.50. I managed to get a hair cut every two weeks and still have a little pocket change left, I even had enough money to give ten cents to the church every Sunday.

The puppet show was a big hit at the assembly and the operetta was also successful probably because I had no major part in it, just one short solo. On the very last day of school the drama teacher asked Paul and me to wait a minute. When all the students had left she told us she was going to display all the marionettes in a book case in her room. This was the first year she had tried to have a puppet show. She told me that I should go see the principal as soon as school was out. She then put her arms around Paul and me and said in a kind of squeaky voice, "I am sure going to miss the two of you." I looked at her face and saw tears running down her cheeks. The school year ended for me when I went to the principal's office. They handed me my report card and a sealed envelope and a small cloth bag and told me to give it to the counselor when I went to school next year. I ended school with a B average and was looking forward to the summer where I could finally get enough sleep.

I decided to try again to find my mother. The bicycle was paid for and I had a little money in my pocket. my clothes were acceptable and my shoes were still in good shape. I decided to tell Mr. William's first so he could get a replacement in time for me to teach him the route. It took one week to find a reliable replacement and two weeks to teach him. Mr. William's informed me that if I ever need to deliver papers again that he would give me first choice when there was an opening. He did understand why I wanted to find my mother. One week before I was to turn the route over to the new boy Harold, I informed Mr. Olson of my decision and would be leaving in about one week. He wished me luck and said I should stop by the house before leaving. The next thing I had to do was tell Paul and his parents what I was going to do. They asked me when I was going to leave and I told them that my last night at the dairy would be Sunday night. I was to meet with the Olsons Sunday evening, wash the bottles and leave in the morning. They asked me to stop by before I left town. The Olsons said if I ever needed a job washing bottles to look them up and they would do what ever they could. They had a nice dinner and invited me to join them. I got a big hug from both of them when I left. I washed the bottles and went to bed for a good nights sleep.

Monday morning I stopped by to say goodbye to Paul and his folks. As I was leaving I asked Paul to go outside with me, he complied but with a kind of hurt look on his face. I told Paul that if I didn't find my mother that I would be back. I handed him a note I had written and put in a sealed envelope and told him to give it to his parents. The note said I was leaving the bicycle with him until I returned. I told Paul to please take it to his parents now and I would wait for him. As soon as Paul went into the house I high tailed it out of there as fast as I could so he wouldn't see me leave. I ran a couple of blocks then slowed to a fast walk. I stopped on what looked like a main street. I didn't know which direction to go so I just stuck out my thumb trying to get a ride. After about an hour a car stopped for me. The man asked me where I was going and I told him I wasn't sure where to go but I was looking for my mother. He asked me where I had last seen her and I told him about my step father and that I heard that my Mother had left him and I didn't know where she went. He told me to think about where some relatives lived and go look for her there. He only gave me about a five mile ride. I caught several short rides and still had no idea as to which direction I should go. I eventually ended up on highway 99 going north from the Los Angeles area.

I caught a ride in a produce truck going to Bakersfield. When we got to the summit and stopped for refreshments and to exercise our legs. I was so proud that I could pay for my own donut and drink. After a few minutes we continued to Bakersfield. We stopped in the outskirts at a packing house, shook hands and said goodbye. I walked a couple of miles to the down town area and stopped right in front of the police station. A policeman called to me and I went over to him. He asked me where I was going and I told him I was looking for my mother. He asked her name and if she lived locally. I told him about her leaving my step father and I didn't know where she went. He asked me where we lived when my father was killed. I told him Yuma, Arizona. he suggested that I go there and see if she went to see some of their friends and they might be able to help me. I asked him which direction I should go and he took me into the police station. They showed me a map of the western states and showed me the roads I would have to take. I was a long way from Yuma and decided I had better get going. I said goodbye and left.

I started walking in the direction I thought I should to go and eventually found my way to the highway, stuck out my thumb and got a ride with a nice couple. They wanted to know about me. I told them about my school year and how much I enjoyed it. I also told them about my going to Yuma to see if any of the friends my parents had would know where she might be. The couple was a minister and his wife who had been transferred to Yuma. They asked if I ever went to church and I said, "Yes." Then I told them about the holly roller church. They got a laugh when I told them about my being scared there and leaving early. I had a great time talking with them. When we arrived in Yuma they gave me the address of the church where they would be. I wondered around town and eventually found a place to eat.

The ride from Bakersfield to Yuma took several hour with only a few stops to buy gasoline. One time we stopped in the middle of the desert at Gila Bend Arizona. There you could get all the free water you could drink to cool yourself off and also water for the poor over heated cars. There was also a covered place where about 3 cars could park in the shade. We had been driving with our windows open but we were sill hot. When we were no longer thirsty we continued on to Yuma. I was kind of sleepy but all of a sudden I woke up as the road became very rough. We were going across the part of the desert that is nothing but large sand dunes. We were on the part of the road that was made from railroad ties. Finally we reached Yuma and I could start my search the next day. I found a restaurant and purchased a sandwich and drink. As I left the restaurant the couple that had given me the ride saw me and stopped to inquire as to where I was going to sleep. I informed them that I hadn't decided yet but that I would be O. K. They didn't want to leave me but I insisted that I would be just fine.

I wondered around not really knowing what to do. I must have walked for a couple of hours. I eventually came to the High School where my Dad was killed. I looked around in the dark and could not recognize anything. I curled up in the doorway of the main entrance for the night, covered myself up with my blanket and slept through the night. The sun woke me early in the morning and I started walking around the school grounds. It took me several minutes before I saw the place where my Mother, sister and I were sitting when the big whirl wind came up. I remembered the sound and the screams coming from the unfinished building. The memories of that day came to me in a rush. I looked up and in my mind could see the exact place where my Dad was working when he was killed. I ran to that part of the building and with my fists doubled up began beating on the building, the tears streaming down my face. I don't know how long I was there but I fell to the ground exhausted. Eventually a custodian found me, he sat down beside me and stared talking to me. He wanted to know what my problem was. Between sobs I told him the story of my dad being killed there. The man stayed with me for a long time until I had a little better control of my feelings. The man did not know of any friends of my parents and could not tell me where we had lived. He pointed me in the direction of town and I headed there. I came to a police station, went in and tried to find answers to my questions. Part of the problem was that I was still to emotional to remember names. No one there could help and wished me luck as I left. I went to the restaurant and ordered a sandwich.

I must have looked really bad as they made me produce the money before they would serve me. I decided to eat just one meal a day to conserve my money because I didn't know how long it would take me to find Mom. There wasn't much left of the day and I still had no plan. I walked in the direction of the train station. I wondered if the Indians still danced for the people on the passenger trains. I suppose they danced to earn a little money from those well enough off to ride the train. There were no trains in sight so I went into the station. I first went to the rest room and looked in the mirror and saw how bad I looked. My face was covered with tear streaked dirt and my hands had blood spattered all over them. I cleaned myself up as much as possible and went into the waiting room. I asked the man behind the counter about the Indians and he informed me that they were usually there in the morning hours. I was also informed that the station would close in a few minutes so I left. As I was walking outside I looked around for a place to sleep and finally spotted an old shed that was open. I looked inside and found it to be empty except for a few spiders and some old rags. I took one of the rags and cleared off a place for me to lie down.

I awoke in the morning to the sound of a locomotive hissing steam. It was bright daylight so I went towards the station. The train was a freight train and I saw some empty freight cars but my search in Yuma was not complete so I did not try to jump into one of the cars. I went into the station and asked when a passenger train was due and was told in about half an hour. I walked outside and saw some of the Indians in full Indian dress beginning to arrive. So many of them looked skinny and under fed. When the train arrived I watched them dance which brought back more memories as my Mother used to take me there to watch and they invited me to join them. I had learned three different dances, rain, fire and worship. I watched them dance for a short time but had to leave there with my emotions getting the best of me again. I asked several people if they knew Al and Josie White or the Highfields. No one could give me a positive answer so I decided to go to the Post Office, surely they would know of them as they must have received some kind of mail. At the post office they could not give me an answer as I did not have the addresses. Well so much for getting answers.

I decided to take the advice I had received in Bakersfield and head for New Mexico. The one thing I did know is that I had to get out of Yuma as my emotions were getting the best of me. I remembered the map I had been shown in Bakersfield If my memory was correct Mesa would be in the right direction for New Mexico. I headed in that direction. I found my way to the main road stuck my thumb out and waited for either a car or truck to come by. I had begun to think that what I thought was a main road was actually deserted. A couple in a Model-A Ford finally came by and stopped for me. They were headed in the right direction but were not going the entire distance but were willing to take me as far as they were going. I decided to take them up on the ride as it was better than just standing there and perhaps another place would be better. They talked quietly with each other for four or five minutes then the lady looked at me and asked if my name was Jones. This got my attention, they might be able to

66

help me. I told them that my last name was Jones. The lady then asked me if my father had been a carpenter and my answer was yes. They knew him from work and church but did not know where we had moved to after his death. I told them that we had visited some relatives in Texas and New Mexico before going to Corona California where my Mother met the man that eventually became my Step Father. When I finally let them talk they told me that I looked just like my father and were surprised to see me, stopped to pick me up to make sure their eyes were not deceiving them. As we drove along we talked about the time when we lived in Yuma. They thought very highly of my parents. The more we talked the more I wanted to find my mother. They took me about half way to Mesa when they told me they could go no further as we were close to their home. They stopped their car to let me out and they both got out and came over to me. The man gave me a big hug and the lady not only hugged me but kissed me. This brought tears to my eyes. The man wrote their name and address on a piece of paper and handed it to me. I told them I would let them know when I found my mother. As they drove off I felt very much alone and for a while I just stood there. I was now very sure I would keep looking until I hound my mother. I waited for the rest of the day without even seeing another car. I found a low place and put my bed roll down. I had a hard time going to sleep remembering the conversation and so many memories of my parents. Being very hungry didn't help.

I woke up in the early morning when something kept hitting my feet. When I opened my eyes I saw a man standing there kicking my feet. He was tall and skinny with a beard and long hair and dirty worn out clothes. He had a knife in his hand and demanded that I give him my food. When I told him I had no food he took my bed roll and scattered my belongings on the ground. I was scared of what he might do next. He sat down next to me and started crying. This really caught me by surprise, I was expecting to have to fight for my life but now I had to calm a man down and I didn't even know the problem. When he had control of himself he explained his problem between sobs. He had not seen his wife and children in two years. He, like so many other men had looked for work in the area where they lived but found nothing. His wife was cleaning the house for a store owner whose wife was having to spend all her time in the store to keep things going and could earn two bits ($0.25) a day for cleaning the house. He left home in hopes of finding work some place else. As time went on and he had found nothing, he was too ashamed to go home with nothing so his wife could support him. I asked how long it had been sense he had heard a radio. He said that it had been at least two years ever sense he had left home. I told him about listening to the radio at the dairy and that I had heard about President Roosevelt getting the W. P. A, program going. He replied that the government hadn't helped in the past and doubted if it would do any thing now. I said it might help if he looked into it, then dropped the subject.

I was getting very hungry and decided that we should look for something to eat. He got angry again and said there was nothing to eat around here in this dry country. I put my bed roll back together and told him that I would be back in a few minutes. He looked at me puzzled and just sat there. Several yards away was a large clump of bushes and so I headed for it all the time being as quiet as possible. When I got to the bushes I saw nothing but sat motionless for a long period of time. I finally saw a little movement but waited for the animal to come closer. When it got into view I saw it was a fully grown squirrel. I watched it until it got closer then threw my knife at it. I hit the squirrel in the neck which stopped it long enough for me to grab it. I hit it behind the ears which killed it, skinned and cleaned it. I took it back to where the man was sitting. He saw the squirrel and jumped up with delight. He wanted to eat it raw but I convinced him we should start a fire and roast it. We gathered some dry grass and a few twigs. I started a small fire with the flint and stone I always carried. We looked around and found a long skinny stick and a few pieces of wood that would make a nice fire. When the fire was going good we put the squirrel on the long stick and proceeded to roast it. The man grabbed the cooked squirrel and proceeded to eat it. I asked for some and he gave me a couple of legs. Well this was better than nothing and I remembered the man had told me he had nothing to eat for the last couple of days.

I gathered up my bed roll and went out to the street to look for a ride. The man went with me. After standing for a long time with no vehicles coming we decided to start walking. We walked for a long time with the man telling me all the places he had been. I told him about my looking for my mother. We finally quit talking and kept walking, each with our own thoughts. There were only two cars that passed us and slowed down as if they were gong to stop, but after taking a look at us they continued on their way. Late in the afternoon we saw a farm house in the distance. The man decided to go there and see if he could do some work for them for food. I said goodbye and good luck then reminded him of the W. P. A. program. He said no more and left me. I was relieved as he left because I thought about the cars that slowed down and looked at us but probably did not like what they saw so kept going. I thought that if a car came by I would have a better chance of a ride if I was by myself. There were no more vehicles the rest of that day. I stopped in the late afternoon when I saw a large stand of brush and decided to find something to eat. When I got to the bushes I saw a pond of water and thought I might be able to see a parry chicken, but no such luck. I saw only a few bugs in the water. Evidently it was just a low place that caught rain water. I decided to wait to see if any animals would come drink out of it. I hid myself in the brush and waited. Finally I saw a pack of coyotes coming. I stayed very quiet hoping they would not see me. If there was a squirrel around I was sure they would find it. But if they were looking for food they would look in the brush. I wasn't sure what to do now. I very quietly took out my knife and waited. A couple of them came in my direction and I was scared. Then the pack decided to leave after having their fill of water. I waited for a few minutes then put my knife away. I did not see any animals or birds. There was some vegetation that I might be able to cook and eat. I cut off some leaves that looked lick spinach and tasted one. It didn't taste too bad so I went to my bed roll and retrieved my tin can and got some water. I gathered some of the small brush that seemed to be dry and started a fire. I boiled the water then rinsed the leaves in it. Got some fresh water and cooked the leaves in it. They kind of tasted like spinach but at least I had something in my stomach. As the sun was going down I heard a little noise in the brush and quietly went over to see what it was. It was a small bird that quickly flew away. I decided the best thing for me to do was to sleep, perhaps in the morning I could find something. In the early morning I went back to the brush and still found nothing so I headed to the road where I would possibly get a ride.

Finally a small model T truck stopped for me. The man had a few boxes of butter milk and eggs he was going to sell to a grocery store in Mesa. I asked if he wasn't afraid the butter would melt in the heat of the day and he told me that he had been on the road sense before sun rise so he could get to town before it melted. I asked how he got so much butter. He said he had a small farm with 8 cows and more chickens than he could count. He has a very large butter churn, so big they can not turn it by hand and it sits in a small pond in their back yard. They divert water from a near by creek to keep the pond full of cold water. The churn has two long boards mounted on the top like a big X. They use four dogs harnessed to the boards. The dogs are trained to walk around in a circle and churn the butter. The store cuts the blocks of butter into the size they want. The man also had some fried chicken and a couple of tomatoes. He gave me a drum stick and thigh along with one tomato. Boy that sure tasted good. After a couple of hours we arrived in Mesa. I helped him unload the butter and eggs and thanked the man. He wished me good luck and good hunting as I looking for my mother.

I walked to the edge of town and waited for a ride. There wasn't a shade tree for me to stand under and it was hot. I waited but no vehicles came by going in the direction I wanted to go. I did see a few cars going to town. Most had families in them. As evening approached I decided to look for something to eat. The area beside the road had been plowed at one time and there was no crop growing on it. As I wondered around I saw lots of the vegetation like I had seen the day before but this vegetation had yellow flowers on it. I picked a bunch of the leaves and looked around for some water but I found none. I ate several of the leaves and they quenched my thirst besides putting a little something in my stomach. It was now getting late afternoon so I found a place to put my bed roll down. I had a hard time going to sleep as I was trying to make plans. Then I remembered this was Saturday. That evening I saw a few cars going in the direction of town. They were mostly families, but a couple of them had young adults that were dressed very nice. They were heading into town for the usual week end entertainment. I decide the young adults were probably on a date. There were no cars heading out of town so I laid back down to sleep. Much later the sounds of cars going by woke me up It was probably the same cars I saw going to town in the evening. I went back to sleep and woke fairly early in the morning, put my bed roll together and headed back to town to try and find a church. I saw a restaurant and decided to get a glass of milk and ask about a church. I went in and headed to the restroom where I washed my hands and face then slicked my hair down with water. I ordered a class of milk for 2 pennies and the nice lady gave me a cookie too. I asked where the nearest church was and the kind lady gave me directions.

I found my way to the church and arrived just as the doors were opened. I stood around until people started arriving then found myself a seat where no one else was sitting.

There seemed to be a special atmosphere as the people seemed kind of excited. As the service began the preacher introduce four men as the Wheeler family. They were traveling to Arizona to sing at a Christian convention. They were a great quartet and sang several of the old songs. Then they sang a new song that no one had heard before, "Glory Land." When service was over I got up to leave but was stopped as a few people came to great me after they had said goodbye to the Wheelers. They asked me where I was from and how I got there. I explained to them about my looking for my mother but, really didn't know where to go except to perhaps find some relatives in New Mexico. One lady and her husband were quiet until the others began to leave. They invited me to have lunch with them and their children. I accepted so we walked a short distance to their house and walked in as the door wasn't locked. There was chicken, mashed potatoes with gravy and vegetables. Boy that was good. The lady told me I should go in the back room where she had heated some water and put it in a wash tub and take a bath. She handed me some coveralls to put on when I was through. When I was finished she invited me into the kitchen where there was pie and milk waiting. After we had fished eating the children, one girl and two boys one of the boys who was about my age asked me what it was like to be out on my own and I told them that it wasn't much fun. I told them about riding freight cars, eating hobo stew and watching out for the bulls and some one trying to take advantage of you. I told them about the man with a knife wanting my food that I didn't have. I went on to explain that I was always hungry and thirsty. That it wasn't always easy to find a squirrel or snake to eat and birds were hard to catch, that the leaves of some of the weeds would quench your thirst. The lady was gone for a few minutes then returned with my clothes, nice and clean and ironed too. After I had dressed the lady and man asked me to spend the night but I declined as I wanted to be on the road as early as possible. Besides I was so full I don't think I could have eaten another bite and I am sure it would have been offered. As I was leaving the man shook my hand and wished me luck, the lady gave me a big hug. The girl and younger boy said goodbye and the older boy walked out front with me. He told me he was glad that I came and shared my experiences with them. He had thought about running away because his parents expected him to do lots of chores and watch his younger brother and sister. He thought they were too strict but after hearing what it is like out on our own he decided he would stick it out until he got older. The boy stuck out his hand, shook mine and said please come back some time and let me know how you are doing. I left there feeling sad that I had to leave such a nice family and friendly town.

I went to the main street leaving town and waited for several hours before seeing any vehicle. A commercial truck stopped for me and said he could take me as far as Casa Grande so I jumped in. The driver was an older man that seemed very friendly. We talked for quite a while before he asked me what I was up to. I told him about looking for my mother and he seemed satisfied with that. He would point out different plants and rock formations as we drove along. I was again getting quite an education. We stopped in Tucson late at night. I thanked the man for the ride and started looking for a place to sleep. At the north end of town I found a low place where I would be protected from the weather, put down my bed roll and was asleep very shortly. I woke up early morning and started to look for food but none was to be found. I went to the road and waited a long time. A few cars and trucks passed but no one stopped for me. As I stood there I heard a train whistle.

I decided that perhaps a train would be a better bet. I finally found the freight yards and looked for a steam locomotive that was headed in the direction of Tucson. There was one sitting there with steam escaping from the cylinders that drive the wheels. It wasn't moving so I skirted around the depot so it wouldn't look like I was going to get on. I hid out in a grove of cotton wood trees and watched the train for a few minutes. I could hear the locomotive building up steam. As I watched I saw a couple of men heading for a freight car. They were running and three bulls were hot after them and finally caught them and were beating them with their clubs. I made my dash to a freight car that had the doors open, jumped in and moved some boxes and hid behind them. The train started moving with a lurch. As the train picked up speed I settled my self down to a more comfortable position and was soon fast asleep. I woke up as the train came to a stop. I carefully looked outside and saw the sign that said Tucson. I was hungry but I stayed put as I wanted to go to New Mexico and in a few minutes the train started moving again. When the train stopped in Lordsburg I decided to get off and find something to eat. I carefully looked outside and seeing no one around I jumped out and ran away from the train. It was really too late to see very well so I found a place to put my bed roll down, I didn't sleep very well as I was so hungry but stayed under my blanket for the night.

Early morning I was up and looking for food. I soon spotted some pigeons in the brush. I was able to capture one but the noise scared the other birds away. I stood vary still waiting to see if the noise had alerted the bulls but none showed up. I cleaned the pigeon and found a place that looked like a hobo camp under some trees. There was a sort of a fire pit and a few sticks in a pile next to it. I built a small fire knowing that the smoke would be dispersed as it went through the tree branched and leaves. About the time I had the fire going five men were standing around me. I looked up with a surprised look on my face and the men said, "got you!." Now I was really confused. They all began to laugh and explained that they had been sleeping further back in the grove of trees and smelling the fire decided to come see who was there. Seeing a young kid they decided to sneak up on me. It wasn't very long before they had a good fire going. They went back to where they were sleeping and gathered a few cans of food and a bucket of water. They told me if I would share my bird with them to put it in their stew they would share their food with me. Sounded like a good deal to me. They had seen me get off the train the night before and were on the look out for me. They were all tired and dirty looking and asked me how I could have such clean and pressed clothes while traveling on a freight car. I told them about the nice family in Mesa Arizona. They asked why I didn't stay if they were so nice. I told them about my search for my mother. They all had suggestions like putting an ad in the paper or over the radio. I told them I didn't know where or how to put the ads in and besides I didn't have any money. We ate the stew and they got a big laugh over my tin can and bent spoon.

I put my bed roll together, said goodbye and headed towards town. I went in several stores and asked if they knew of the Rocking N cattle ranch. My mother's oldest brother Oakley owned a cattle ranch some place in New Mexico. No one seemed to know about it so I figured that my Uncle Oakley must live in another part of the state. This took most of the day so I headed back to the freight yards. I went back to where I had met the men but they were gone. I hunted around for a while and found where they had gotten the water. It was a small artesian spring. I found the large pot and cast iron skillet that they cooked the stew in it was hidden away so others passing this way could use it. They were also too big and heavy to carry in a bed roll. Looking further I found the trash they had left behind and there was a squirrel scrounging for food. I took out my knife and with a lucky throw I hit the squirrel in the neck which paralyzed it. I killed it, cleaned it and built a small fire where I roasted it. The day was basically over so I decided to stay put and catch a train the next morning. I felt warm and secure in this grove of trees where others had stayed for a while. In the morning I looked around and found a snake sunning its self. So once again I had something to eat. There was also some wild mustard growing a few feet from the artesian well. The leaves from the mustard greens cooked up nicely although they didn't near fill the pot. I cut the snake up in about two inch pieces and fried it in the skillet. After eating I cleaned the pot and skillet so I could return them to where I found them. The skillet was really hard to clean as I only had sand and water. While cutting the snake I noticed that my knife was getting dull. This meant that I had to find a smooth sand stone to sharpen it. I looked around the artesian well for a stone that had been polished by the running water. I found one but it wasn't very good, but it did sharpen my knife. It was now getting late in the morning and I really wanted to get going.

I headed back to the freight yards to see if there was any thing going on. Every thing was very quiet. It looked like no one was around so I headed for the nearest open box car. I jumped in and hoped no one would come check on me. A little while later a bull looked in the box car and saw me. He did not jump in and start beating on me but rather called me to the door. I went over and sat down. He asked me if I knew how dangerous it was to be playing around on a train. I told him that I was looking for a ride to Deming but had no other way to get there. He wondered why and I explained that I was looking for my uncle's cattle ranch and that I only knew his name and brand. I didn't even know the name of the town where he got his mail. The man told me to leave the train yard and if he saw me there again I would get the club used on me. I took my bed roll and headed back to the grove of trees to decide what I should do next. It wasn't an easy decision. Should I chance the freight train with this man looking for me or try to find the road to Deming? I decided to try the road so I headed away from the train depot. The main road usually followed the train tracks so I was sure I could find it. Sure enough there it was about forty five minutes walk. I waited for a vehicle for a long time before a car finally showed up and stopped for me. I wasn't sure if I should accept the ride as it was the bull from the train yard. He motioned me to get in and said he was headed in my direction. He drove for a couple of hours then stopped in the middle of no where. He asked to see my bed roll and I handed it to him. He rummaged through it and said there is nothing to steal here then reached across in front of me, opened the passenger door and tossed my things out He ordered me out of the car and told me to start walking. I got out and started putting my things together. He turned around and headed back to town. I now wondered what to do. There were no more vehicles that day and it seemed like I walked a hundred miles even though I knew it was only five or so miles. I finally saw a bunch of trees about a mile away and headed for them. I bedded down for the night and again tried to decide what to do. I was so hungry I could have eaten anything only there were nothing to be seen. I was almost to hungry to go to sleep and had to control myself so I wouldn't cry. I finally went to sleep and woke up before the sun came up. I once gain looked for something to eat but found nothing.

A couple of hours later I saw a man on horse back coming in my direction. When he got to me he asked how I got so far out in the country and I told him about the bull at the freight yard. He told me to hand him my bed roll and climb up on the horse behind him as the horse could travel faster than me and I looked like I was already tired. As we went along we made small talk then he reached in his pocket and pulled out a harmonica and began to play some western tunes. He asked if I liked music and I said "yes very much so." He played a few more tunes then started to make sounds like a locomotive whistle. It was a very mournful sound and made me wish I had hidden from the bull and caught a freight train. We rode for several hours then spotted a ranch house that he said used to belong to him. He lost the ranch about two months earlier because people could not buy the beef he raised so he had no money. The only thing he had left was the horse, saddle and the few clothes he had with him. He said he had saved every penny he could to buy this place and as soon as he could afford it he and his girl friend were going to get married. Now all his dreams were shattered. He had no food but did have a canteen of water which he shared with me. Late afternoon we stopped where there was a little grass for his horse to eat and bedded down for the night. I told him

I would look for an animal or snake in the morning. When we woke up in the morning I started my search after telling him I would be back in a few minutes. Sure enough I saw a snake hiding in the grass where the sun could reach it. I decided that if there was a snake around there must be a small animal some place close. I stayed quiet for several minutes and all I ever saw was a couple of mice and I didn't want them. I finally killed the snake and we were able to gather enough grass and dry weeds to make a fire to roast the snake. This was the first time he had eaten snake and decided it was pretty good. He asked how I killed it and I told him with my knife. He wondered how I got close enough to kill it without getting bitten. I told him how the Indians had taught me to throw my knife then pulled out my sand stone and showed him how I sharpened it. He seemed to like what I told him and asked if I could teach him. I told him that it would take a lot of practice and asked if he had a knife which he did. There was nothing to set up for a target but I did explain how to hold the knife and throw it. We heard a vehicle coming our direction so he told me to get out there and see if they would stop for me while he led his horse away so it could eat some grass.

The car did stop and offer me a ride but asked about the man and horse so I explained how he had given me a ride the day before. The couple invited me to get in and I heisted long enough to wave goodbye to the man and he saluted me. They were going to Las Cruses if I wanted to go that far. They were using the last of their money for gas and hoped it would get them all the way so they could join relatives that lived there. I got in the car which didn't sound like it was running so good. Very shortly we started going up a slight grade. It took all the car could do to make it to the top but it made it. A little while later there was a much steeper grade and I didn't think the car could make it. I told them to let me out so the car would have that much less weight and it could probable make it. I pushed on the car to help it get going up the hill and it finally got up enough speed that I couldn't keep up with it. I waved goodbye and watched as they disappeared around a bend in the road. I heard a steam locomotive struggling to get up the hill and I headed towards it. When I caught up with it I was out of breath but the train was going very slow. I jumped on the ladder at one end of a freight car and waited till I could catch my breath then jumped off again hoping I could see an open box car. Sure enough an open car appeared down the hill a little ways away so I headed for it. The train was still going very slow and I easily jumped into the car. There was no place to hide so I got back out of the day light as much as I could. Shortly after that the train topped the hill and started picking up speed so I was safe for the time being. The train slowed down at Las Cruses and stopped on a siding. The car I was in started moving again before I could even get to the door to peek out. I stayed put to see what would happen and the car was put on a siding. It was disconnected and I figured I had better stay put as there would be employees around. Very shortly the car was connected up again. As the train started moving I got brave and looked out and I was glad to see the tracks were headed North. I was once again safe for a little while. To my surprise it never stopped until it arrived at Vaughn. I looked out and there was no one around so I got off and headed for the usual grove of trees but this time they were eucalyptus trees. These trees will grow in the hot climate with very little water. It was late at night so I found what looked like a place to sleep. No use looking for something to eat in the dark. It was so dry and hot I didn't need to cover up. In the morning I searched around for something to eat but found nothing.

I walked into town and located a restaurant, went inside and asked to see the owner. The man I was talking to wanted to know why. I said I would like to sweep the floor or wash dished and maybe even wash the windows. He said, "I am the owner and no I do not want you to work." I was told to go into the restroom and wash my face. When I came out there was a plate with hot cakes, an egg and some bacon. I explained that I didn't have any money and he barked at me, "EAT." When I was through eating he came over and sat down beside me. He told me that his son had left a couple of months earlier as he didn't want to wash dishes or help in any way so they had an argument and here I was willing to work for food. Then the questions started so I explained my situation and asked if he knew of the Rocking N Cattle Ranch. He had no knowledge of the ranch and did not know any Oakley, so again I was left with no answer. I thanked the man for breakfast and went looking for other stores where I might get an answer to my questions. After searching most of the day I was ready to call it quits and head home as the summer was half over and I didn't know how long it would take me to find my way back to Clearwater and locate Mr. Olson. I found the main road heading south and hoped for a ride.

I saw a boy a little younger than me coming in my direction. I waited to see what he wanted and asked why he was there on the main road. He said the one thing he knew was that he had to leave home. His father had lost his job at the freight yards and there was no money to buy food or anything. His dad was always angry with him and told him to leave. I asked him his name and he told me it was Lester. It looked to me like he had a very small bed roll and I asked him to show me what he had. He unrolled his blanket and there was one shirt and nothing more. I could see he had lots to learn about living out in the open. He rolled his blanket up and we started walking down the road. He was very sad and I had to find a way to cheer him up. We started walking and for something to do I started whistling. I remember my mother could whistle better than any one else I knew. After a short time my lips got tired so I decided that maybe a song would be better. I encouraged Lester to help me make up a tune and words. He caught on very quickly and we had fun making up songs. We had only walked a short distance before we saw the freight train yard. I decided that maybe he should learn how to get on a freight car without getting caught by the bulls or getting hurt. As we approached the tracks I told him about the grove of trees that was always close to the freight yards. We went over to the trees and watched as a train started to move. About this time we saw four men heading to a freight car but they had waited to long and the train was picking up speed. The men started running and we saw two of them get in a fright car. The other two men were a little behind them but a passenger train came through and blocked our view. When the passenger train had passed and no one showed up to check we could see something by the tracks and decided to take a look. There might be something that Lester could use in his bed roll. This was a big mistake as there was nothing Lester could use. The only thing to see was parts of a man's body on the tracks. Blood and body parts were all over the place. I almost became sick to my stomach and Lester actually did get sick. The other man was no where to be seen. Lester saw how dangerous it was and I asked if he would like to wait for the next train and I would show him how to get on a freight car. He told me that he never wanted to get close to a train again, so we headed back to the grove of trees and watched as men came and started removing the body parts. We waited for a while then because most of the day was gone we decided to spend the night in the grove of trees. I asked if he was hungry and of course he said yes, I searched around for quite a while then spotted some quail. I was able to kill one of them before they flew away. After waiting several minutes the quail came back and I killed another one. I showed Lester how to clean them, then started a fire and we each had one. We had nothing to drink, but decided to go to bed. Early in the morning when we woke up Lester said he was cold so I loaned him my leather jacket. He felt much better after this. I looked for food again and found nothing so we headed for the road. I kept wondering how he had been able to eat and sleep, he said that he would go up to a house and beg for food. Sometimes the people were nice and would give him something to eat but many times he got yelled at and told to leave. While we were walking back to the road we saw a wind mill off to one side and decided to go in that direction. We walked across the dry and dusty field that hadn't seen rain in a very long time. There was no grass or even weeds growing. When we reached the wind mill there was a tank which caught the water as it was pumped by the wind mill. We used my tin can and took turns drinking then splashed water on our face and hair, scrubbed our hands a little then headed for the road. We walked for most of the day making up songs and laughing when our songs were silly. I asked Lester several times if he wasn't too hot with the jacket on and he told me that he never had a leather jacket and keeping this one on made him feel good. Late in the afternoon a car stopped for us and the people said there was only room for one of us. I told Lester to accept the ride. I thought I could take care of myself better if I was by myself. The car was long out of sight before I remembered my leather jacket but it was too late then. I could use that jacket in the mornings when it was cold and was sorry to not have it any more.

I continued walking down the road. I found very little to eat and every time I passed a wind mill I would go to it, look for something to eat but found very little. I at least had water to quench my thirst. I thought it better to walk than to just stand in one place. I knew I wouldn't be able to walk the entire distance to Clearwater but I had to do something. I eventually saw a bus coming towards me and going in the direction I wanted to go, it was a Santa Fe Trail Ways bus. I didn't expect the bus to stop for me but I put my thumb out anyway. The bus did stop and the driver motioned for me to get in. I explained that I did not have any money and he told me to get in any way. This was my first time on a bus and boy was it comfortable and I didn't complain even though I was hungry. Some of the people had their lunch with them and I watched them eat. No one offered me anything so I just sat there looking out the window. We headed towards Santa Fe and as we drove along we got to see many beautiful sights along with the dry land. There was one place where we stopped and the bus driver ate his lunch. He offered me a sandwich and drink of water which I gladly accepted. While we were stopped the diver took us on a tour of a place known as the Sky High Pueblo.

The Pueblo of Acoma, known as Sky City, sits on a 365-foot-high rock in New Mexico. It's considered the country's oldest inhabited village—archaeologists estimate American Indians settled there about 1150.

Sky High Pueblo

This looked like a place I would like to explore and maybe sleep in but would have to wait for a later year. After a short time we got back in the bus and headed for Santa Fe. So many things to see and so much sleep to get caught up on. In Santa Fe I thanked the driver for the ride and asked why he had picked me up. The driver finally asked me why I was out on the road and said he had picked up several children while driving the bus. He didn't expect to see me walking along the deserted road. He hadn't seen any other vehicles that day. He was glad to have some one to talk to and point out the different things along the way.

In Santa Fe I decided to head West toward Albuquerque. I spent the night in the bus depot and no one bothered me. In the morning I went to the edge of town and looked for something to eat. In this dry area I could find nothing that I recognized so I decided to head out. As luck would have it a truck stopped for me very early. The driver was friendly but drove the entire distance to Albuquerque so I slept a great deal of the time. Albuquerque was a major freight terminal. I didn't want to be stranded on the road again so I decided to try the freight train again. It looked like there were more cattle cars than any closed freight cars. I scouted around and finally saw a freight train starting to move in the direction I wanted to go. I worked my way between cars that were standing still so no one would see me. I finally saw a couple of cars where the doors were half open. I caught one that had some boxes in it. I settled down for the ride and about that time some one closed the door. I waited for several minutes and tried to open it but it would not budge. There was nothing I could do but sit back and wait. I dozed some and began thinking about all the things that might happen to me. I was afraid that the door would be opened and a bull would beat me or have me thrown in jail. My mind went crazy with all kinds of horrible things that might happen. I could no longer sleep with these thoughts. Finally I came back to reality when the train came to a stop. I waited what seemed like an eternity and finally the door was opened. No one looked in so I got out as soon as the coast was clear. I only got about 50 feet away when some men with large two wheeled carts showed up and started unloading the car. I decided that I had enough excitement for the time being and started looking for the road leading out of here. As I was starting to leave I saw the corral where the cows are held before loading them on the cattle cars. Next to the corral was a large stack of hay for feeding the cows. I decided to look for an animal that I could eat. Sure enough there was a group of rabbits. I threw my knife and stunned one. I was able to capture and kill it. I looked around for some water and in the corral there was a water tank for the cows. I scooped some in my can. Then I had to build a fire. The only thing I saw that looked like it would burn was the hay. I didn't want to use it as it was feed for the cows. I looked around and saw some dry cow dung. I knew this would burn so I gathered up a bunch of it and went to a bare place where I could start the fire. I washed the rabbit in the tank and cut it up so some of it would fit in the can. After starting the fire and broiling the rabbit I got some more water and a hand full of hay. I boiled the hay and it didn't taste too bad. When I had cleaned my can and gotten a drink of water I headed for the road. But looking back and seeing the corral gave me an idea. I headed into town and started asking the clerks in different stores where the nearest ranches were located. Most ranches were several miles out of town.

I went back to the road and as luck would have it an old pickup was coming in my direction. I stuck put out my thumb and the driver stopped and asked me where I was going and I told him that I was going to the different cattle ranches to see if I could get a job. He informed me that the ranch where he worked was getting ready for a cattle drive and they might be able to use me for a few days. It took about three hours to reach the ranch. The ride took long enough for me to tell of my traveling around. At the ranch I was introduced to the owner a Mr. Boone. I explained to him what I knew of our family and our relation to Daniel Boone. He said, "any Boone was good enough for him, ". He had me ride a horse to see how well I could handle it. He was pleased with what he saw and said I could help on the cattle drive which would take about five days if I would accept good food for my pay. I thought about it for only a minute then replied very loudly, "YES." At least I would eat good for a few days. The company of the cow boys, their stories and the GOOD food off the chuck wagon made it all worth while. At the end of the cattle drive I said goodbye and went back to the road to continue my trip. There were no vehicles in sight so back to the train station It was. I caught the first train heading in the direction I wanted to go. Later when the train stopped I looked out and saw a sign that said I was in Gallup and another sign that pointed to Winslow. Great I was headed for Arizona. I got off the train to try and find a little food. but soon came to what looked like the main road

85

so I decided to try and get a ride. A short time later a car stopped for me. They were headed for Gallup New Mexico. That was on the way to Winslow so I was happy for the ride. The usual questions were asked about my being on the road. They volunteered information about them selves. They owned a hardware store and had hired a couple to watch it for them so they could take a vacation. They had no children so they couldn't understand why some one would order their kids out of the house. We had only driven a few miles when they spotted a combination restaurant, gas station and a small zoo that advertised they had baby rattlers on display. We stopped and they purchased donuts for all of us along with a drink. We went out to look at the snakes. They were not what we expected. Instead of live rattlers they were actually rattlers made for babies. After laughing about this we got back in their 1932 Dodge and continued on our way. The country side was very bare with little to see but as we watched the scenery began to slowly change. We could see signs of where the Indians had lived and the irrigation ditches they had dug to water the plants they grew. As the day went on our conversation was more about their business and this was their first vacation sense the crash in 1929. The man was getting tired of all the driving without stopping to rest. I felt sorry for him and said I could drive if he wished me to. With a surprised look on his face he pulled over and asked me when and where I had driven. I explained about driving my step father's truck when I was 10 years old and that Mom had allowed me to back our Model-A out of the garage and turn it around. He asked his wife if it was all right and she nodded yes. He asked her to get in the back seat, put me in the driver's seat and sat down in the passenger's seat. I asked him to show me the shift pattern and started the car. As we drove along he began to relax. I was driving so there was no more chance to look at the surrounding area. I noticed that they were soon both asleep. As we approached Gallup I woke the man up. He was confused for a couple of minutes, sat up straight and shook his head. He then looked at me with a grin on his face and told me I had been doing a great job. I stopped the car and got out so he could drive. When I stopped the car his wife woke up, so I got in the back seat and she got in the passengers seat. As we drove along he spotted a motel and stopped. He asked me where I was going to stay that night and I said I would find some place to sleep. He started the car again and drove a little further to a restaurant. They invited me in to have dinner or as they put it supper with them. I tried to refuse but they insisted I go in with them. I went into the bathroom and cleaned myself up a little and when I came back I spotted them at a table with a place set for three people. They had been discussing me and decided I should stay the night in the motel with them. We went back to the motel and got a room with an extra bed. I was kind of embarrassed to be sleeping in the same room with them but they insisted. We talked a little then listened to the radio. As I sat in the chair I started nodding off. They woke me up by saying I guess it's time for bed as it has been a long day. I was asleep before they were even in bed. I was the first to wake up in the morning so I took a shower so as to be out of their way. They took me back to the restaurant and bought me breakfast. What I didn't know was that they had been talking about going on a little further and looking at the Petrified Forest and wanted to know if I would like to go? I told them about my having to get back to Clearwater but they insisted and promised to take me a little further if I went with them so of course I agreed. We got in the car and drove to a gas station and I cleaned the windshield for them. The ride to the Painted Dessert was a long one and I shared driving with the man. It was getting late in the day when we arrived at the Petrified Forest but was still early enough for us to look around. I saw one log lying on the ground that looked like a very long bench and I went over and sat down on it. The lady came and sat down beside me, put her arm around me and the man took a picture. We then went to the town of Winslow where they once again they put me up for the night.

In the morning after breakfast they said that we were going to look at the Painted Desert. All I could think of was how great a ride this was. After spending several hours we headed back to Winslow. They purchased my dinner and had me stay at a motel with them. They told me that they had gone as far as they could and would now have to go back home and to work. I was sorry to have to say goodbye. The lady hugged me and the man shook my hand and I headed for the road sad to see them leave.

My next destination was Flagstaff. I at least was starting out with a full stomach. The sun was straight over head when a cattle truck finally stopped for me. I saw the truck was empty and the driver looked tired. He was happy to have company and welcomed me to get in. I soon learned his name was Jim. I told Jim about the nice people that had given me a ride and took me sight seeing. They even bought me food and had me sleep in the motel. I told Jim that I sure enjoyed living like that. He explained that he had just taken a load of cattle to Gallup and was headed back to Flagstaff. As we traveled along it was interesting as the landscape changed from desert to lush green trees. He told me many stories about the early days of Flagstaff. He was born and raised in the area. It was very late when we arrived but he knew of a restaurant that would be open. He purchased dinner for both of us; we then got back in the truck and drove to a parking lot big enough for his truck. He asked me if I wanted to sleep on the seat of the truck as it would be better than out in the open. He took his keys and locked the door after telling me I could open it from the inside. He asked me to wait for him in the morning that there was part of the old town he wanted to show me. I bid him good night and watched him walk away then covered myself up and was soon asleep. The next thing I knew he was waking me up and we went to a nearby restaurant where he purchased breakfast for us. All I could think of was that I have had a really neat time the last few days. When breakfast was over we walked to what he called the old part of town. Sure enough there were old stores with paint that was flaking off. He pointed out the old general store where you could buy most anything. There was an old barber shop and next to it was a saloon where there used to be dance hall girls and so it went for a couple of blocks. All the time I was fascinated by the wooden side walks. I asked about them and he explained that the road was not paved in the early days and when it rained or snowed the street was muddy. The side walk was built so the women could walk on it and not in the mud when they did their shopping. When he got through showing me around he took me to a restaurant and bought me lunch. Boy this was great. After we left the restaurant he told me that if he ever had a son he hoped that he would have good manners like me. I really didn't know what he meant. I didn't even know which side of the plate the knife and fork went on. He then wished me luck and that he had to go to work.

It was still early afternoon so I headed for the main road going towards Wickenburg. I did not wait very long till I got a ride from a family that was going to Prescott. I thought it would be a fun ride as there was a girl and boy about my age. Boy was I surprised. The kids kept complaining about being crowded and it was too hot, or I want a drink and so went the afternoon. I tried to talk to the kids but they told me to shut up as they didn't want to talk to a tramp boy like me. The parents tried to talk the kids into being nice but they would have none of it. As we road along I tried to ignore the kids put they persisted in being rude. There was so much beautiful scenery but no one could enjoy it. I was glad when we arrived in Prescott. I asked to be let out at the edge of town so the car was stopped and the parents apologized to me for the rude behavior of the kids. It was getting dark so I decided to find a place to sleep. I wondered around and the only place I could find that had some shelter was in the door way of the post office. I laid down on top of my blanket and thought about the day. From luxury to insults. When I woke in the morning it was cold and getting light. I was hungry and wondered where I could find something to eat. I started walking through town and as I approached the outskirts a lady came out of a store and motioned for me to come inside with her. She said "you must be cold with no sweater" and I nodded yes. She went to a clothes rack and picked out a sweater that would fit me. I told her I had no money and she told me to forget about paying for it. She then walked me across the street to a restaurant, spoke to the waitress for a few minutes then told me to tell them what I wanted to eat. Again I said I had no money and she told me to look at the sign above the door. The sign read, "GOOD WILL industries." She explained that the Good Will helps people in need. All the items were donated and they could afford a meal for some one really in need. She told me that she knew I was in need as I had a bed roll with me so obviously I had no home. I had a good breakfast and went back outside, a little warmer in the cool morning air. I went in the Good Will store and thanked the lady. I then headed down the road hoping for a ride to Wickenburg.

After waiting most of the day with only a couple of vehicles going my direction I decided that maybe the train would be the best way, and I had heard a couple of locomotives whistle so even though I was fearful but school season was rapidly approaching. I decided to try catching a freight train again. I headed towards the direction of the train yards. I looked for a freight train headed in the direction I wanted to go. I saw a train headed in the direction of Wickenburg but it was going too fast for me to catch. I was too far away from the train station. I walked along the tracks till I saw the train station. It was late in the day so I decided to wait until morning before hitching a ride. This was a wooded area where I was sure I could find an animal or bird. I soon spotted some quail I killed one and roasted it over a fire. A train whistle woke me in the early morning so I hurriedly put my bed roll together and ran towards the tracks. I saw a freight train headed towards Wickenburg. The train was picking up speed so I threw my bed roll in and started to jump in, about that time something picked me up and pushed me in. I turned around and watched a man jump in behind me. I asked if he had pushed me in and he nodded yes. When the man caught his breath he told me that he couldn't let me end like a kid did the day before. I guess I looked puzzled so he told me about a boy a little younger than me that had tried to get in a freight car when the train was moving too fast and he lost his balance. When he got to the boy he saw that the boy was badly injured, one arm was almost completely cut off and there was a nasty cut on his head. When he tried to help, the boy was still able to talk and kept yelling, "don't take my leather jacket." The boy yelled this a couple of times then passed out. The boy died before help could arrive. I learned that the man was a railroad bull but he didn't believe in beating young people. He would rather try and help. We talked in general about his job, my looking for my mother and what I was going to do next. When we arrived in Wickenburg he helped me off. We went into the train station and I was afraid he was going to have me arrested but instead he took me into a room set aside for train personnel to rest for a few hours before they would have to go back to work. I slept through the night and when I woke up he was gone. I left the building and started looking for something to eat. Before I knew it the railroad bull caught up with me. He grabbed me by the arm and said, "no you don't, you don't get away that easily." I was afraid he was going to arrest me and tried to pull away. He had a paper bag in his other hand and thrust it towards me. He told me to sit down and open the bag. I sat down immediately and opened the bag which had an egg sandwich in it. After I was through with the sandwich I was told to go with him. Now I knew I was really in trouble. He led me to a large truck and told me the drivers name was Don.

Don was a long distance truck driver and was going all the way to Los Angeles. The bull then handed me $5.00 and told me to buy food for myself so Don didn't have to pay. I didn't want to take the money but he told me it was a belated birthday gift from his kids and they would be unhappy if I did not take it. Don drove all day stopping only to get something to eat and rest for the night. He let me sleep on the seat of the truck and he went inside where there were bunks set up for the drivers. Each time I tried to pay for my meal he would not let me. He told me over an over again that I would need the money when we got to L. A. It took us 3 days to travel that distance. When we reached the warehouse where he had to stop he wished me good luck and pointed in the direction of Clearwater. It was late in the evening so I found a place behind some parked trucks where I would be out of sight. In the morning I headed for the road leading in the direction Don had pointed.

It only took a couple of days to reach Clearwater but it was late afternoon so I went into the restaurant and got a bowl of Chile. The waitress recognized me and seemed to be pleased to see me again she had a friendly smile and greeting. I went to the place by the red car tracks where I had stayed before and slept through the night, feeling save to be back in an area I knew. In the morning I went to the dairy to see Mr. Olson. Both he and his wife welcomed me with open arms. I was informed that they did not have a job for me washing bottles as they had hired a man with a family to support. I wasn't sure what to do at that point but told them I would be all right. I picked up my bed roll, said I would be back to pick up my other things as soon as I got settled. I went to see Mr. William's. He told me that he liked the way I worked and thought that perhaps he could help me find a job as there were no paper routes open at that time. He drove me to a small dairy in Bellflower and introduced me to John and Carolina Smith who were the owners. They also had a 3 year old boy, "Richard."

I was shown a room with bathroom facilities and they would bring me my meals. I was to bottle milk and be on hand from 8 A. M. until 10 P. M. to sell milk to customers. I also had to watch Richard when they did not take him with them. I had to be on hand all the time so I couldn't figure out how I could go to school and church. Larry the man that tended the milking machines and fed the cows was not happy with his job and I could understand why. Richard was a real pain to take care of. He thought he could do anything he wanted while his parents were away. If I tried to reprimand him he would threaten to tell his parent that I was mean to him and he did one time. His parents really scolded me and threatened to beat me if I ever did it again. Mr. William's came to check on me after 14 days and I explained every thing to him including that I did not get paid, The Smiths told me that room and board was all they could afford He went in the house and returned in a few minutes, told me to get my things together and go with him. On the way back to his place he told me of another dairy in Compton and the owners said they would like to talk to me. I spent another night with the Olsons and in the morning Mr. William's took me to the dairy in Compton.

The owner was Mr. Tom McLarin and he was very friendly. He explained that Mr. William's and Mr. Olson talked very highly of me and said that I was always there on time and that I did a good job. The job was to bottle milk for four hours in the morning starting at 4 A. M. and again in the afternoon from 4 P. M. to 8 P. M. The pay to start off with was not that great $0.10 an hour but it would do until I found something better. Mr. William's took me to a restaurant and bought me lunch then took me back to the dairy. I started to work that evening and met the man that took care of the cows and milking machines. Jack was a nice man. He was married and had two children. He liked me right off the bat and asked where I was staying. I told him that I would sleep where ever I could find a sheltered place to put my bed roll down. Jack said that he would talk to his wife as they had a spare bed room. He asked what I could pay and I told him how much I was to be paid. He said that was a nice start and the owners were nice people and if I did a good job he was sure they would give me a raise. When I finished that night I walked around the dairy and the only sheltered place I found was in the door way of the dairy. I decided to sleep there and hoped I would wake up early enough to get to work. In the morning Jack woke me up. He told me he thought he would find me there and he came early so he could help me get stared. As I was getting things ready he helped me and also told me that I could have room and board for $2.50 a week, they hoped to get $4.00 but being that I didn't get paid that much they would settle for the $2.50 until I got a raise. The $4.00 included laundry. Jack said his wife was not really happy getting only $2.50 but they were sure of getting the money as I would be working the same place as him. That would leave me little money for the week but that would do as long as I had a place to sleep and food to eat. I accepted the offer immediately. Then he added one more thing. He could drive me to and from work as he worked the same shift. I was in luck as I now had a place to stay, food to eat and there was still a few days before school started. He took me to his home after the morning shift and introduced me to his wife Phyllis and their two children Alice and Donald. Every one was nice to me and I explained that I had to go get my things from Mr. Olson. We first had something to eat then Alice showed me the room where I was to sleep. One thing I noticed is that the house was very clean which made me feel so dirty and shabby. Jack offered to take me to see Mr. Olson but I told him I would like to rest a little first. I went to my room and Phyllis knocked on my door and told me to give her my clothes and she would wash them for me. I handed her my clothes through the door then laid down to rest. When I woke up I found my clothes clean and pressed just inside the door of my room. I got dressed and went to find Phyllis. She was in the living room watching her children who were working on a puzzle. I thanked her for taking care of my clothes and told her I should be going to see Mr. Olson and get my things. She told me that Jack was still asleep and couldn't take me at that time. I told her that I thought I knew how to get there and besides I didn't want to disturb Jack as he needed rest. I went outside and looked around so I would know how to find their house when I returned. I had never been in this area before and had to search around for quite a while before I found the road that I thought led to Mr. Olsons but nothing looked right. I decided to go back to the house and try another time. When I found my way back to the house Jack was up and offered to take me to the dairy. This time I accepted the ride. When we arrived at the Paramount dairy Jack seemed to recognize Mr. Olson. I found out later that Jack had gone to school with Mr. Olsons son. The two of them had a great time talking about their families and completely forgot about me. It was getting late and almost time for Jack and me to go to work. I cleared my throat and brought them back to the present time. They said goodbye and promised each other to visit in the near future.

Jack took me straight to the dairy as it was getting time to go to work. I enjoyed watching the machinery work as this was the first time I got to watch modern equipment. I would turn the turn table and pull a handle. As 3 bottles were being filled with milk I would place 3 clean bottles in pockets on the turn table. So 3 bottles were being filled, 3 bottles were receiving the paper cap and I was placing 3 empty bottles in the 3rd section. Fascinating for me to watch so the evening went fast. On our way home I asked Jack to show me where the local High school was and he drove a couple of blocks and pointed out this school that was larger than any I had gone to, he was sure that was where I would go. It was such a short distance that I knew I could walk there after work. Before we went to work in the afternoon we would have an early dinner. Phyllis was sure a good cook. On Sunday afternoon we went to the neighbor's house where all the children were together having a great time with a puzzle and I was invited to join in. This was fun having a family where I was invited to take part in their games. Before I went to work the next morning I got my report card and the envelope I was given last year. After work I told Jack that I would go and try to register for school. He told me he would take me and sign for me if it were necessary. Jack went in with me and helped me pick out the classes I would take.

The counselor read the letter I gave him and nodded his head as though he understood, then gave me a very serious look. I wondered what it was about. Jack signed for me and went out in the hall with the counselor. Jack and the counselor came back into the room. The counselor shook my hand then with a big grin wished me luck. When we got in the car Jack told me that the letter explained my situation and that they recommended me to be accepted as I was not a trouble maker. This didn't take long so Jack took me home and explained to his wife what had transpired. It looked to me like this was going to be a good year even though I hadn't found my mother. Jack and Phyllis were fun to live with, to top it off they went to church so after the morning shift Sundays they took me to church with them. And still another plus was they had a piano and I was allowed to play it when ever I wanted. Some afternoons Phyllis would play the piano and sometimes I would play it. We all stood around and sang our favorite songs. Some mornings after work jack would take me to a nearby restaurant where I would purchase a hardy breakfast. Jack was surprised as I ate as much as he did and he teased me about how fat I was going to be.

One Saturday Jack took his kids and me to a vacant field and taught us how to make a kite. He had purchased some thin sticks of wood, glue and 3 balls of string. We used news paper to cover the kites. We spent all the time we could flying our kites, mostly Saturday afternoons. One day I decided to try something new as my imagination was working full speed ahead. I took a piece of paper and made a hole in the center of it, slipped it over the sick which held my ball of twine and watched it as the breeze carried it up to the kite. In my imagination I was sending a message to people on my kite. As time went on there were more and more children coming to watch us fly our kites. Some of the children came with store bought kites and some had nothing.

I showed the children with no kites what they needed and as soon as they showed up with the material I would teach them how to make a kite. I soon had quite a following as they all thought I was an expert. Most kites worked fine but every once in a while a wood piece would break so I learned how to make smaller kites from the broken pieces.

School was in process and I had asked to be in the band. The band instructor thought I should be in the orchestra as I played the piano but I insisted on the band. I wanted to be in the marching band. I was assigned to the drums where I started with the snare drums because I could keep the timing right. After about one week the teacher asked me if I ever played a wind instrument and thought maybe I would like to try one as I could read music. I was assigned a baritone which was easy to play due to the large mouth piece. I just had to learn how the three valves worked. I was allowed to take it with me after school so I could learn the correct valves to use for the different notes of music. I got pretty good at it and after about a month. The teacher then asked me if I wanted to try the euphonium and I agreed as it looked like it would be fun. The Euphonium was a funny looking instrument as it had two bells and two extra valves one valve sent the music to the trombone bell and he other one to the baritone bell. It didn't take long before I had mastered the valves. We marched in a few parades, fun! I also took wood working where I made a small magazine rack. I passed the school year with average grades except for band where I got an A, I was thinking more and more about my mother. I told the kite flying kids goodbye then headed for the dairy and told Tom I would be leaving in a week. Jack was next on the list to hear what I had to say. I told him that I was going to go back to the Tule Indian Reservation to see if I might get a clew from them by something I might have said. He wished me luck and said they would welcome me back at any time. The week passed quickly and as I gathered my things and tied my magazine rack on the bed roll I said my final goodbyes. The thing that bothered me most was that I never had a chance to go see Paul. He was evidently in a different school.

With my bed roll and pack on my back I headed for the road leading towards Los Angeles. There was enough traffic that I expected to get a ride almost immediately. No one stopped for me, so I decided to walk a little further. I would walk a couple of miles then stop and put my thumb out. Finally a milk delivery truck stopped and I got in. The man recognized me as the kid that had shagged bottles for him a few years before. He insisted on taking me to lunch so I could tell him about my adventures. After lunch he took me to the main road through Los Angeles heading north. I soon got a ride with a couple in a coup with a rumble seat. They were going to Bakersfield and that pleased me. They had a daughter (Ruth) in the rumble seat. I threw my things in and jumped in beside her. Street car tracks ran down the road the same as cars. I watched the street car that was behind us. Each time the signal arm that said stop came up I would keep a careful eye on the street car. It would get so close that I thought it might hit us. Eventually the street car turned on to another street and I could relax. Ruth had a blanket and as the evening hours became cool we leaned against each other and covered with the blanket. It was still light when we started on the ridge route to Bakersfield.

Ridge Route

It was a very narrow road and at times you would be right next to the edge of a cliff. Made it scary at times. There were times when there wasn't hardly enough room for cars to pass each other going in opposite directions. It was cool in the mountains and Ruth and I were glad to have the blanket. The man kept driving at night because it was easier on the car engine. We finally stopped at Gorman for a quick bite. I was glad I could pay for my own food. The man drank a couple of cups of coffee before he was ready to go on. It was morning before we stopped again at the place called Grape Vine. We finally got to Bakersfield about noon. I hated to leave but they were home and I still had a ways to go.

I walked for a while before I saw a truck stopped by the side of the road. The door was open and the driver was laying on the seat with his feet hanging out. As I was passing it I heard the man groan and I asked if I could help. The man, Jack had been driving from Los Angeles to a packing house close to Terra Bella which was in the direction I thought I needed to go. He asked me if I could drive a diesel truck. I had never driven a diesel and wasn't sure what the difference would be. Jack told me the main difference was in starting the motor.

99

You had to first start a compressor to pressurize the cylinders. When the air was compressed it would get hot enough that the diesel fuel would ignite. I told him that with his help I would drive him to Terra Bella. The truck transmission had five speeds forward and a three speed transmission behind that. You had to use all the gears to keep from lugging the motor and damaging it. So I learned to use all fifteen gears. When we arrived at the packing house there was another load of produce that had to go to Los Angeles. Jim asked me if I would help him deliver it as if he couldn't they would find another driver and he could loose his job. It was still early in the summer and I decided I would have enough time to help him and still get to the Indian reservation.

The truck was loaded that evening. There was a driver's waiting room at the packing house. We got a ride to Terra Bella and found a restaurant that was open. He purchased dinner for me and got himself a bowl of soup. We found a ride from a farmer back to the packing house and found chairs we could sleep in. I had my pack so I had something to cover up with. In the truck was a small blanket for Jack I woke early in the morning and woke Jim to see how he felt. He still didn't feel good but thought we should get going. I started the truck and we headed back to the highway. There were four sharp turns before reaching the straight stretch to highway 99 and Bakersfield. Each time we approached a turn I would have to shift to a higher gear ratio. This took several maneuvers as I had to go through all the gears to protect the motor. We reached Bakersfield and thought it would be good to eat something. We stopped at a restaurant and I had a hardy breakfast, Jim had a bowl of cereal. As we walked out to the truck he got sick again. I didn't know what to do except keep going. This meant I would have to drive the ridge route. I stopped at the bottom of the ridge route at The Grape Vine to check the truck over. The next five miles were a 6% grade and would be hard on the truck. I headed for the long pull gathering as much speed as I could before starting up hill. The truck did its best but it kept loosing speed on the grade. I eventually was in first gear. The truck was going so slow that I could walk by the side of it, stepping on the running board to correct directions. Jack would occasionally wake up and check things. At times you could see bolts or screws fall to the floor from the dash board. They would come loose from all the vibration. I stopped behind other trucks at the summit to check the truck. Jim woke up and told me what to check. I went in the restaurant and got a hamburger and milk. It was late at night but I was awake and the produce needed to be delivered as soon as possible so I started over the rest of the ridge route. I was very tense as passing the few vehicles was a tricky thing as the road was so narrow. When I started down hill towards Burbank Jim woke up and seemed to be feeling much better. We stopped at a restaurant that had enough room for trucks and ate breakfast. I was finally relieved of driving and could sit in the passenger's seat until we got to the produce warehouses on Alameda Street in Los Angeles. It didn't take long for the truck to be unloaded and I was glad as I was very tired. Jim was feeling so much better that he suggested we head back to Terra Bella as soon as we had eaten. The trip back was uneventful as Jim was an expert driver. He drove most of the wave over the ridge route then was tired enough he asked me to take over the driving. When we arrived at Terra Bella Jim asked me to wait a minute. He went into the office and soon returned. He handed me $50.00 for helping him and wished me luck. I tried to refuse that much money but Jack insisted. I started walking towards town and as I was passing a service station I saw a fuel truck unloading. Painted on the side was a flying horse and the address of the supply company in Porterville. I went up to the driver and asked if he was heading back to Porterville, he replied, "yes." I asked if I could get a ride. He looked at me and my bed roll, laughed and said I looked like I needed a ride. On the way he asked me what I had been up to. I started telling him about my driving for Jack, He recognized Jack from my description and said he was a good man with five children to support. I was now really sorry I had accepted so much money from him but was informed that the $50.00 was a small price for him to pay as I had probably saved his job. When we arrived at the edge of Porterville he let me out and said, "Good luck and thanks for the company."

HOME AT LAST

I decided to go into town and get something to eat before heading to the Indian reservation. I was looking around for a place to eat and as I looked across the street I saw Mom coming out of the Safeway grocery store. I looked for cars coming from both directions, I only saw a couple so I dodged between them, ran up to Mom. When she saw me she dropped the bag of groceries and we gave each other a big hug. Not far behind her was Grandma and my two sisters Georgia Lee and Neldafae. Mom threw her arms around me and cried. Georgia Lee and Neldafae hugged and kissed me. Grandma waited her turn then came up to me and said, "I knew you would show up sooner or later you come from strong stock." I picked up the groceries and carried them to the car, a Model-A Ford, 1929. Mom and Grandma got in the front, Georgia Lee, Neldafae and I squeezed in the back seat with my bed roll, magazine rack and the groceries. Georgia Lee was still the prettiest girl I had ever seen. I'll bet she sure was popular in school.

There were many questions asked and I just kept talking. When we arrived at Grandmas house I recognized it. It was really great to be home again. Yes I knew there was lots to be done. I spent the first couple of days around the house then started visiting the neighbors. We went to church on Sunday and there were still people I knew. They made a big fuss over my being home and had lots of questions.

102

Home
Grandma, Georgia Lee and me at Porterville, Ca House

I thought to myself that I had been so close when I was at the Tule Indian Reservation when I first started looking and didn't know where to look. There was now a bathroom in what was once a bed room and running water in the house. We spent all day catching up on the latest news of the family. The memories of Grandma and us kids (Georgia Lee, me and cousin Irma) helping to clean up the yard and plant new flowers for Grandma all came back. Grandma had five acres with several chicken houses and a fenced back area for the milk cow. It was fun to be home. Mom took me to town the next day and wanted to buy me some new clothes. I had heard her telling to Grandma and say she really didn't have enough money to pay the electric bill let alone buy me new clothes but she thought the store might let her pay a little at a time. When we picked out the shirt and jeans I showed her the money I had in my pocket. She wanted to know where I had gotten the money and I told her about my driving the truck. We then went to a shoe store and I got a new pair of shoes, I handed Mom the rest of my money except for one dollar. She tried to refuse it but I wouldn't take it back.

103

Sunday we went to church and every one was glad to see me. J. E. Wheeler even took us to Holts Malt shop to celebrate my coming home. I had lots to learn about the routine and kept busy cleaning the chicken houses and many other chores. Mom told me that with Dad and Grandpa both gone I had to be the man of the house. The first thing I had to do was get things cleaned up around the property then I could go look for a job. I had a few days before school started so I spent the first week getting things in order. We had to go to the store for groceries and buy gas for the car. When we stopped for gas I talked to Mr. Oran Shela about me working for him. He asked how much I knew about cars and I told him what little I knew. He told me that due to Moms reputation he could hire me for Saturdays and Sunday afternoons, the pay would be seven cents an hour to start and he would train me. If I did well at the end of thirty days he would raise my pay to ten cents. So far so good I was HOME and had a job just in time for school to start.

In school the first class I selected was band. The teacher was Mr. Robinson, the same band director Mom had when she went back to high school. I chose English and the teacher recognized right away that I was a good reader, probably due to Mom having me read the Bible as soon as I could read. Mom had me read part of the Bible every day. I chose the gym class then American History. I was really interested in American history as I thought I really knew a lot due to my travels. Little did I know about it though, There was lots more to it than where I had been. Next I chose Public Speaking and social studies I thought this would be easy as I could tell about my travels. I rode the school bus to school and back but it seemed to take such a long time as it went to all the farms around the area. The first day I rode the bus, Georgia Lee got on the bus first and sat up front. There was a seat next to me in back and a student I had seen walking with crutches sat next to me. He told me his name was Floyd Powers. Floyd asked me if I knew the girl up front as he would like to meet her she was really pretty. I knew right away he was talking about Georgia

Lee and told him it was my sister. Floyd and I became life long friends. There was lots of work to be done at home and I needed all the time I could get to do the work. I decided to try walking to school save time. It took me about 30 minutes less time to walk than the bus took so it was a good idea. There were chickens and pigs to feed, eggs to gather up and a cow to milk. I also planted half an acre of Chinese cabbage to feed to the chickens. I started making friends at school and even saw a cute girl that I wanted to get acquainted with. I asked Mom if I could use the car once in a while and she told me we would have to talk about it as Georgia Lee used it every Friday night. After a lot of discussion it was agreed that I could use it every other week. This gave me enough courage to go up to the girl and introduce myself and she told me her name was Dorotha Leonard. I asked her for a date to the school dance but she told me that she already had a date and I would have to ask her sooner than just a couple of days before I wanted to take her out. Friday one of my new friends asked me if I knew that Dottie was having a birthday Saturday and there was to be a party at her house. Jim told me that if I would meet him in town he would take me there. I was excited as this would give me a chance to get to know her. I asked Georgia Lee what I should get her and not knowing Dorotha (Dottie) the only thing she could think of was a box of candy. Well this was better than nothing but while buying it the clerk suggested a bottle of Channel #5 perfume to go with it. A little more than I wanted to spend but I wanted to impress her. Jim picked me up as promised and it didn't seem to matter that I wasn't invited. I was as welcome as every one else. When Dottie opened the present she gave the present giver a kiss. When she got to mine there were two presents. She kissed me and I said, "don't I get another kiss? I brought two presents." Without hesitation I got a second kiss and a far better one than the first one. The evening went by too fast and my spirits were high. On the way home Jim teased me about having a crush on her, I couldn't deny it. It seemed so easy to get my work done at the garage and again at home. It was like my feet never touched the ground. Monday at school I looked for her and again asked for a date, this time she accepted. I even managed to find her and have lunch with her. I just had a mustard sandwich and small container of milk but it was enough. I noticed that she just had a sandwich also. We talked a great deal and I learned that she loved to sing and I told her about my love of music. The next day I asked Mr. Robinson if I could talk to some of the other students about starting a band and he thought it was a good plan He would even loan us the instruments if we needed them. I found enough students interested to start making plans for our band. I would be the leader and we could practice for 1/2 hour after school in the band room. We got good enough that Mr. Robinson approached the principal for us to play at the next assembly. By now Dottie and I were a couple in all school functions. I asked her to join us after school and she could do the singing. Dottie and I would sing most of the popular songs. We finally got good enough that we played for the school dances and even played for the Lions Club a couple of times. One night at the school dance we sang the song, "My Desire" (at least that's the name I remember). I had the band play it again and I talked it adding a few words all the time looking at Dottie, "I don't want to set the world on fire baby I just want to start a flame in your pretty little heart. In my heart there is just one desire and that one is you." This went over great and we were asked to do this at several of the dances and school assemblies. About two months later some of the students heard one of the big bands talking a song and adding a few words like I had done. The band continued playing at dances until the end of the year. Roscoe Honeycutt and Ynema were always together. Ynema was a close friend of Dottie's. Every Friday was date night, Roscoe, Ynema, Dottie and me. Roscoe would drive one week and I would drive the next. Often we would park by the side of the road, turn the radio to one of the big bands and dance in the street. We were into the big band mode most of the time. On Sunday Mom would allow me to go pick up Dottie and bring her to church with us. After church I would take her home, then head for work at the garage. In Gym class I tried all the different sports. I was selected as center in basketball but was too short so I didn't do so well. Next was baseball where I was good enough at short stop to play on the team. Football was what I really wanted. I could play but not on the school team as I was too young and small. One day while practicing a foot ball was kicked in my direction. Watching the ball I didn't see Richard coming towards it too. We collided head on. I walked around dazed for a while but poor Richard was knocked unconscious and just laid there for several minutes. He eventually began to recover but played no more foot ball that day. In my senior year I was finally old and big enough to play on the school foot ball team. I played quarter back as I was the fastest one on the team and did a pretty good job. My band got together as often as possible. We all had chores to do at home and some of us had jobs but we managed to practice and play at dances quite often. Sometime on holidays we would go to a park and enjoy swimming in the river and just enjoying being together.

August 1941 was coming to a close and it was time to get ready for my senior year at Porterville Union High School. I had spent most of the summer working for Oran Shela. He owned the Oldsmobile agency along with a garage and service station. I changed tires, pumped gas and lubricated cars. We had the reputation of being able to lube a car and the springs would not squeak for 1,000 miles (quite a reputation to uphold). Dottie and I continued dating all summer. We double dated with Roscoe and Ynema. Roscoe would drive one Friday and I would drive the next. We could each use the family car every other week. Dottie and I kept my band going all summer by playing for dances at the Lions Club every couple of weeks. In school I was able to sign up for most of the classes I wanted, Automotive Repair, Band, social studies and public speaking. I had to take English and gym. There was always news of the war in Europe with the Nazis going into so many different countries. The bombing of Great Briton seemed to be constantly in the news. We also heard very often about Max Schmeling and his boxing as he was the world heavy weight champion. Most of us were too busy to worry about happenings in a foreign country. The teachers were intent on us learning what they had planned for the year The English teacher introduced us to many old poems. She always asked me to read them to the class. I was quite good at reading.

Mom was working in a packing house but always found time to help me. She would help me prepare sermons and practice them. The church we went to was very small and could not pay a preacher. A farmer would preach one Sunday and I could preach the next Sunday. Mr. Wheeler led the singing. Every Sunday evening Mr. Wheeler would quiz all the young people on the bible, challenging us to find chapters and verses. He would also spend time teaching all the teen age boys to lead songs. Our Church was known for it's singing. During the summer the church would advertise that we were going to have a pot luck with lots of singing. Many people showed up, probably around 150 from churches in the surrounding towns. Mr. Wheeler owned a furniture store and also took care of the church business.

Mr. Robinson the band instructor was very helpful as he always let my band members borrow the instruments they needed. He also arranged for us to play at the school sports functions and march in parades around Tulare County. Social studies was about what we could read in the local paper (Fresno Bee). Public speaking was always fun as I shined in that due to my experience in church. In Gym I could play base ball and basketball and was finally allowed to play on the school team. I even got to play the lead roll in a school play. About 1 week after school started a new student showed up. He was African American and the teacher kind of ignored him, didn't bring him up to date on the little we had learned. I was working with the drill press and he came over to see what I was doing. I explained as much as I could and asked if he would like to try. After drilling a couple of holes in the piece of metal I had he thanked me and just walked around the shop. From that time on every time he saw me he would come over and talk to me. I thought we had become pretty good friends but one Saturday night I was walking down Main Street and saw him going in the opposite direction. As we passed I said hi to him but he looked the other way. Monday I saw him and asked why he had just walked on without saying anything. He explained that I was with some white friends and if he spoke to me they would probably beat me up. This was the first time I had encountered prejudice.

I was working in the gas station when we got the word that Pearl Harbor had been bombed. It seemed every one in town stopped by to make sure we knew about it. In school the following Monday all the teachers told us what they had learned and you could tell they were afraid of what might be coming our way. Most of my friends were too young for the Army but all of us were ready to help. Activities continued as normal the rest of the school year. My very close friend Floyd Powers and I did our traditional New Years outing. We would go up to the mountains where we knew the river would be frozen. We would break he ice and swim a few feet then get out, dry our self's off and head for town for a good hot meal. Dottie had expected us to get married and her dad told her he would give us half of his farm for a wedding present. Dottie had even purchased a small ring and told all her friends that it was an engagement ring from me. I wasn't sure if I could support her and still take care of my Mother, Grandmother and sisters. I thought that after school was out I could get a full time job and then things would be O. K. About this time Floyd told me about the Merchant Marines and said he would like to go as they might take him and wondered if I would like to go with him. I thought this might be a good idea so agreed to go with him. Floyd had to use a cane when he walked. Here was a chance to help my country and earn enough money to Marry Dottie. But now first would be graduation and all that went with it. Mr. Wheeler bought me my graduation suit. This was my first suit.

My Graduation Picture

I was so proud of this suit. I wore it to the senior Prom, the graduation ceremony and every other place I could think of. When I would get home I was very careful to not get it dirty and press it each time before I wore it. The last date I had with Dottie I told her I was thinking about joining the merchant Marines. She said If I went in the Merchant Marines that she would not wait for me. I hoped she would change her mind as defending our country was so very important.

CHAPTER FOUR

MERCHANT MARINES

The following Monday Floyd and I headed for San Francisco to find out how we could join. When we arrived we didn't know where to go. We saw the sign on a window where you could join the Army so we went in and asked if they knew where the office was for the Merchant Marines. The recruiting soldier asked our age and neither one of us was old enough to join the Army so he gave us directions to the Merchant Marine Union Hall. We went inside the union hall to inquire and saw a man behind a window so we went up to him and asked where we could join. The man asked Floyd about the cane. Floyd said it helped him to walk. We were told that they could not use a man that was not physically able to walk on a ship especially if there was a storm. I was given instruction on how to get a Seaman's Passport and then join the union. Floyd left for home very sad and I told him I would look him up the first chance I got.

I was told that I would be an Ordinary Seaman for two years. The pay was $19.50 a month and that $15.00 would be held back to pay for room and board on the ship. After a full 2 years at sea I would be promoted to Able Bodied Seaman and my salary would be $29.00 a month and the $15.00 would be deducted. If I were in a war zone there would be a $100.00 bonus for each day. I agreed to this and signed for 30% of my pay to be sent to my Mother. The 1st 2 or 3 days they taught me to tie knots in a rope for a while then play checkers. I learned the other men were waiting for their name to be called and told which ship to report to and which dock it was at. I had just learned how to use a bosens chair and was practicing when the San Francisco Chronicle photographer showed up and took my picture. I got a copy of the paper and sent it home to my mother. My name was finally called and I was to report to the S. S. Calamaris which was in dry dock for repairs. I was the 1st deck hand to show up and was assigned a couple of jobs. The next day two African American men arrived. They were what was called mess men. They served food and cleaned up afterwards. Within a week all the deck crew was signed on. I learned that as you signed on the ship you could choose which shift you wanted. There were three shifts of four hours each. At sea you would work four hours on duty and eight hours off. I did not know this so I was assigned the 12:00 to 4:00 watch. This of course was not the best time for me as I had been working from early morning till late afternoon and was always asleep by 12:00 midnight. We helped prepare the ship for sea. We would work an 8 hour shift then had the rest of the time for our self's. Merchant seamen seemed to drink a lot of whisky. Every evening when we were finished with our days work we would congregate in our focsal and talk about the war. One man would open a whisky bottle, take a drink from it and pass it to the closest man to him. When the bottle reached me I tried one taste and didn't like it so after that I refused to drink. Finally one very large man stood up and said, "I am going to beat the **** out of the next man that offers the kid a drink." When the ship was ready to launch I was told to go and get a stopper. I asked where I would find it and was told, "in the foscalhead." The foscalhead is in the bow of the ship and I hurried there not knowing what I was looking for. As I got there an older seaman was working and I said, "Where can I find a stopper?" He answered as he pointed to a messy pile of rope, "in there." He finally came over, reached in the pile of rope and drug out what he called the stopper. I hurried back to the poop deck and arrived just in time as the seamen were ready to haul in the mooring line. The war had been going on long enough that all Merchant ships were outfitted with 50 caliber machine guns and a larger caliber gun mounted on their forward and aft decks. The gun was called a 6 inch 50. We headed for Seattle, WA to load supplies for the Army and Coast Guard in Alaska. Going up the coast to Seattle we were close enough to shore that the ship would roll slightly to the starboard then to the port. The ship rolled quite a bit as they had not attached the stabilizer fins, this allowed the ship to roll even more. Being a farmer boy I had a very hard time staying awake from midnight to 4:00 A. M. I was on stand by and headed to the mess hall where I saw the men playing cards. I asked how they stayed awake and they pointed to their coffee mugs then pointed to the coffee maker. I got the picture and poured myself a mug of coffee. I drank it even though I didn't' like it. For the next couple of days I was almost sea sick from the coffee and the rolling of the ship. Over the next few days I found I could drink the coffee if I used 1/2 cup of hot water and the rest coffee.

In Seattle we loaded ammunition and other explosives. We also loaded two narrow gauge locomotives on deck to take to Alaska. In Juneau we unloaded some of the cargo and the two locomotives. I was surprised to find they could grow strawberries in Alaska. We were in port three days. Each day the seamen who were not on duty would go ashore and visit all the liquor stores and bars. Every evening the Captain would send me into town to herd the sailors back to shore. The Coast Guard was at the gang plank as guards and a couple of the Merchant Marine sailors came up the gang plank smocking. We had explosives on board and the seamen were instructed to put their cigarettes out, but they were drunk enough that they refused. They were removed by the Cost Guard and taken off the ship so we were two men short. When we were ready to leave Juneau there were four other ships headed to open waters This was the first convoy I was in. Two of the ships were torpedoed, all the seamen were rescued according to sparks the radio operator, but both ships sunk. I was learning to steer the ship. There are 360 degrees to a compass and each degree is divided into several points on an ocean going vessel. While going through the narrows if I was more than 1 1/2 or 2 points off the course the Officer in charge would kick me in the seat of my pants hard enough that I would find myself on the wing of the bridge. I soon learned how to correct any movement of the ship caused by current or wind.

In the narrows there are buoys to mark the lane where the ship could go. The Officer in charge of the Coast guard (armed guards) would often have them taking target practice with the 50 caliber machine guns. We Merchant Seamen called him a 90 day wonder. The trouble is he was having them shoot at the buoys. Before we reached Anchorage our steering engine quit working. We ran aground but not hard enough to damage the ship. The steering engine was repaired and we were able to continue on. One day we were waiting for high tide and dropped our anchor to hold us in place. Another young seaman and I decided to take a swim as it was a nice warm day. During the war all merchant ships had life lines draped over the side of the ship so you could get off the ship in a hurry if needed. The other sailor and I dove over board and the water was so cold we quickly climbed back up the life lines. We were then told that a person could live only about 3 minutes in that cold water. Later I understood why as a few hours later we rounded a curve there was a large glacier. Never saw so much ice in all my life. In Anchorage the single dock was about a mile from town. One day I went into town to look around. I found a Drug Store with a soda fountain and got a milk shake, there was also a roller skating rink. I went in and tried to skate but the floor was so warped from all the moisture that it was hard to skate.

From here we headed up to the Aleutian Islands. Dutch Harbor to be exact. The 1st day we unloaded the last of our supplies. We were anxious to get home as we were running out of our food and supplies. There was a storm approaching so we were not allowed to leave. The following day the Japanese attacked with a small group of plains, this kept us in port another day for our protection. The following day a large group of enemy planes was spotted coming in our direction. We were ordered to anchor away from the docks. Our ship was empty and we had only replaced the tween decks (hatch boards) on the bottom deck but were not finished battening down the hatches. As we watched we saw a plane heading towards us. A couple of other sailors and I laid down by the hatch coming. The plane dropped one bomb directly at us. We could both see and hear it. The bomb went into the hold and as it exploded one of the sailors looked in the hold and his head was blown off. I watched in horror as he walked several feet with no head. The seaman was buried at sea as we left port.

We were coming down the coast and as we approached Skagway I was on look out. I heard some one yell Japs. I turned around and looked back aft. There on the main deck was a Japanese pointing a rifle at me. I quickly ducked behind the bull work on the wing of the bridge. I could hear the man coming up the ladder so I hid behind the part of the bridge that is hidden from the wheel house. I had a pocket knife with a 2 inch blade and had it open and ready to use. When I thought the man was too close to use his gun I jumped out to grab him. I jumped too early and he swung his riffle and bayonet at me cutting my left shoulder real bad. In my mind both arms were still working so I grabbed him which forced the gun down and it went off shooting me in the foot. I was cutting him as much as I could and when he fell overboard I tried to grab his riffle for a souvenir but missed. There were no more Japanese on the ship. The Captain sewed me together as best he could without anything to deaden the pain. There was no doctor on board and the captain had some first aid knowledge. My left arm was in a sling so I could do very little work, just stand look out. We continued on towards home, stopping at every place we could and loading canned fish. We had canned salmon or fresh caught salmon for breakfast, lunch and dinner for about 6 weeks as there was no other food. One thing I learned was to sharpen my pocket knife sharp enough to shave with as we were out of razor blades and other supplies. We finally arrived back in Seattle where I was taken to a hospital. The doctors did the best they could which was very little as it had been a long time sense my injuries. I at least got some GOOD food. I was told by security that if any one asked why I limped I should tell them that I had stepped on a fid and hurt my foot. In Seattle we all collected the money we had coming to us and signed off the ship.

I headed for the train station to return to San Francisco and was surprised to find several of the other seamen there. They had purchased new suitcases in which they had their clothes and several bottles of whiskey. It took two days and nights to get to San Francisco. I didn't understand why it took so long. When we arrived I could not find a room so I went to an all night movie theater. They played the same movies over and over again but that did not put me to sleep. In the morning when the bus depot opened I got the first bus I could that would take me to Porterville. The bus stop in Porterville was across the street from Oran Shelas business. I went across the street to see him. We had a good talk then he showed me a 1939 Chevrolet business coup and I could have it for $900.00. I gave him $50.00 for a down payment a tank full of gas was included. I headed for home with my newly purchased car.. When I was almost home I saw Donna Gutherie in her front yard. I stopped and called her name. She looked at me and came running over. I asked her to go to the movies with me that night. In the past if I asked her out she would have to get permission from her mother. This time she looked at me and yelled "Yes," turned, and ran in the house yelling to her mother, "I'm going out with Eddie tonight." I went on home and brought every one up to date on where I had been etc. Mom showed me the post card I had sent from Juneau. The front of the card had a picture of the harbor at Juneau and the notation on the bottom of the card aid it was the harbor at Juneau, Alaska on the other side where I had written (We are in Juneau, Alaska). The word

Juneau had been cut out by the post office. I picked Donna up that evening and we headed to the theater. When we arrived at the theater in front were several of my class mates from school. What I didn't know was the story of our ship in Alaska had been released and printed in the local news paper the day before. Donna and I finally went into the theater but they would not let me pay for the tickets. After the movie I took her to the fanciest restaurant in town and again I was not allowed to pay. During the next several days I could not pay for any thing. I was the first person to return home that had been in hand to hand combat and the first to return that had been injured. I was being welcome as a hero. The main street was about 1 mile long and traffic was always slow on Saturday night. I could not leave the car doors unlocked, all the girls in town wanted to be with the home town hero. I looked up Floyd and we enjoyed our visit. I took him with me when I could I even gave him a ride to the river where we went swimming. I spent one week in Porterville then headed back to San Francisco.

I reported in at the union hall and in less than a day was assigned to a ship the S. S. Lauraline. One thing I decide to do was to study for an officer's ticket. The shifts were 4 hours on with 8 hours off. During one of my 8 hours off I was on deck with some of the other seamen, most of which were either Norwegian or Swedish and all were very big men. The language they used was a mixture of Swedish, Norwegian and English. I always tried to mimic the broken English they used and they usually laughed at me. A Swedish seaman motioned me over to him and told me he had a saying he wanted to teach me so I could tell it to the Norwegian Bosin. I couldn't understand it but I did learn to say, "Teetamonie teetamonie bosman nacha veda pulley zemmy" When I knew it well enough He told me to go tell the bosin. I went over to him and repeated it. I was watching him to see his reaction. I saw this great big ham sized fist starting to come my direction. The Swede called out, "ingateen, ingateen" and the fist stopped in mid swing. The saying is, "Captain Captain the bosin fell down off the mast like a Swedish bird that can't fly. The word ingateen means that nothing was meant by that.

I made sure that I got to know the captain and officers as soon as I could. All the officers were willing to teach me the sextant and other navigational tools. Our mission was to transport troops and ammunition to Pearl Harbor. It was a smooth enough voyage and when we arrived I checked out the Islands at every opportunity. I made friends with the Mayors daughter and even though gas was rationed she drove me around quite a bit. Buildings in town were small and mostly made of wood. Many of the people still lived in grass huts. I never saw so many beautiful birds and flowers in all my life. For our trip home we loaded several caskets with the dead from the Pearl Harbor bombing. These were all placed on the bottom deck of the ship. Most of the tween decks were not put in place. One night we had a little rough weather, I was on the wheel and Red was on standby. The ship rocked just enough for one of the tween deck boards to fall. The 1st mate ordered Red to go below and check on what happened. While He was down there the ship rolled again, enough for one of the metal hatches to clang shut. Red was back in the wheel house in seconds the hair on his head standing straight up, he refused to go back down and check things out. When we arrived in San Francisco I collected my money. When we arrived at our home port I decided to stick around abd see how soon I could get on another ship. I called home and mom told me that my sister had a baby so I went to a baby store and sent a gift. The baby was a girl named Vickie Lynn. I also sent Oran Shela another payment. I called Floyd at his home and he was packing. He had accepted a job as an engineer for a television station in Eureka, CA.

Steam ships were too busy carrying troops and supplies to make a coffee run to Brazil and the fuel oil was used for the war effort, not for coffee. I was given the opportunity to sail on a Full rig Bark. The Bark is a sailing ship where the top mast is square. I made friends with the officers and learned a little more. Our destination was La Paz South America. The ship had a small engine to operate the screw to get us in and out of port. There was also a generator for electricity for lights and water reclamation. There was a very small fresh water tank and it had to be refilled very often. It would take about six months for the trip. I learned how to climb the rigging to reach which ever mast needed attention. I was thankful that we never had rough seas. There was no one that had any hair cutting experience and we had to conserve on water consequently none of us shaved or cut our hair. When we reached La Paz on a dare from each of us to the other most of us got a large ear ring in our left ear. Nothing unusual happened on the voyage. We returned to the U. S. and docked in San Pedro California. The trip had taken about six months. I threw my duffel bag over my shoulder and headed towards town. As I was walking down the sidewalk people would stare at me. My beard was several inches long and my hair was even longer than that. I went into the first barbershop I came to and told the barber to give me a hair cut but leave the beard alone. I was really proud of that beard. People still stared at me so I went back into the same barbershop and had them give me a shave. People still stared at me, it was then I remembered the ear ring. I removed the ear ring and no one even looked at me after that. I saw a public telephone booth and called Thurman and Harriet Wall in Porterville and asked them to come get me I had left my car with them. I knew it was about a six hour drive each way. Thurman had his own business and said that he would close the shop for one day and they would meet me the following day around noon. I went to a movie then got a room in a local hotel. In the morning I just hung around wasting time. Thurman and Harriet finally arrived. I never told them about my long hair etc. They were interested to know how I liked the sailing ship. We had lunch and went back to Porterville. I dropped them off at their place and drove home to surprise

Mom. I finished paying for my car so Oran was paid off now and I would have a little more money. I was glad to see every one but anxious to get back to San Francisco.

I only waited a few days and signed on the S. S. Eva. At least that was the name painted on the bow. I was over the bow in a bosens chair touching up the paint before we headed out to sea. I could see where something had been welded then removed. I swung myself away from the ship several time before I could finally make out the name BLACK GULL. I wondered why the name had been changed but soon forgot about it. In the Merchant Marines there was a lot of superstition. I tried making friends with the 1st mate but he was having none of it. The other officers were friendly enough but I had little time to learn. The captain did loan me a book on navigation. We were headed for the South Seas, just where our destination was I didn't know. As always our ship was loaded with explosives. The 1st mate was a real nasty kind of man. No one liked him but all were afraid to confront him. A few days out to sea we ran into a rather severe storm. The ship tossed back and fourth. It would go over one wave, slide down the side of the wave and dive completely under the next wave. When I reported to the wheel house the next morning I was asked if I knew where the 1st mate was. I had no idea of what they were talking about. I was told that the 1st mate disappeared during the night. I finished my shift and went to the mess hall still wondering about his disappearance. During lunch this was the topic of discussion. The conversation soon turned to the men wondering if there was a jinx on the ship. I wondered what they meant and was informed that when a ship is in dock and the rats left, the ship was doomed. There are other indications of a jinxed ship. I asked if they sometimes changed the name of a ship to remove any jinx of that ship and the answer came back a resounding yes. I went on to explain that the original name of our ship was the Black Gull. There were a lot of questions thrown back and forth.

The older seamen had heard of the Black Gull and superstition had it that on every voyage something bad would happen. Two days later we were sunk by a torpedo. All of us got off alive and into the life boats. We had been adrift 3 days when I was asked to pray for all of us. I guess the way I acted and talked, they figured I was Christian. We lived on what few provisions were on the boat (mostly malt balls) and the few fish that were caught. I was asked to pray for our safety almost every day. Every day there was talk about the superstitions of seamen. On the 22nd day after our being sunk we were picked up by the Navy who took us to sick bay for examination of our health. When we were finished with bones they took us to the mess hall and gave us large bowls of soup. We were given bunks to sleep on. I sure did like this getting pampered the way we were. After a couple of days recuperation we were back to our old selves They took us back to San Francisco. We were once again examined and officials took us into a room and asked us many questions. Did we know what sunk us, what was our exact location etc. When I got out of the hospital I decided to go home and take it easy for a few days. I didn't stay very long as I knew I was needed and headed back to catch another ship.

I was immediately sent to a ship owned by the United Fruit Lines. Due to the shortage of seamen I was to sign on as an Able Bodied Seaman even though I did not have enough sea time. The officers were more than helpful with my learning navigation. The ship was loaded so heavy that it sat low in the water like a tanker. We headed to New Zealand which meant we had to cross the equator. One night when it was very cloudy and dark I was on look out. All seemed normal then off to the port side very close to us I saw a flash of light. Some one had accidentally pushed the black out curtain aside from a passing ship. What scared me was that it had to be another ship so close to us that I could almost touch it. I reported this to the officer in charge but nothing could be done. He was excited about it.

During the war, ships did not use their running lights and merchant ships were not outfitted with sonar so we didn't know it was there until I saw the flash of light. Next day this was all that was talked about. As we approached the equator I noticed that the seas were very calm. They were almost like a mirror. The wake of our ship soon disappeared in the smooth water. One of the engine crew was an African American. One day I saw him on deck and asked why I never saw him up in the fresh air. He said, "Look at the color of my skin. If I stay in the sun very long I get sun burned so I stay below deck. I sun burn a lot faster than you white folk." There is a tradition that when you cross the equator you have to go through some kind of ceremony so you are no longer a soft shell but a hard back. The ceremony consists of what ever the hard backs can think of. There were boxing matches, tying of many kinds of knots. One man that was not easy to get along with had a rope tied around his waist. He was tossed over board and left in the water several minutes before he was drug back on board. He kind of cleaned up his act after that.

Our destination was Auckland where we unloaded most of our supplies. The local people thought we were a tanker and wondered what we were doing there. As the ship was being unloaded another seaman and I decided to see as much of New Zealand as we could. Motor transportation was expensive and not very available. We decided to walk as far as we could and soon came to a riding stable. A lady ran the business. We asked about the horses and she asked if either one of us had ridden before. I told her about my working on a cattle ranch and she said, "Good." She had one friendly horse and another one that the rider had to control. She asked if I had ever used spurs and I told here that on the ranch we some times had to use them. Her daughter brought two horses out. She told me which one to get on then said, "Do you know how to cluck like a chicken?" Her daughter was embarrassed with her mother's noises. I got on the horse she pointed out to me and we headed out to see the country. The horse I was riding tried to knock me of several times by going close to a pole or under a low hanging branch. So I had to show it who was boss. We had a good time for several hours then returned the horses. One thing I noticed was that there were almost no young men. I later learned that all men able to serve in the military were in Great Britain. In the evening we were invited to what they called games. When I arrived there I saw that what they called games was what we in America call square dancing. An interesting thing was that on Sundays and holidays all stores were closed. In fact the day before they would close early.

When we were unloaded we headed for South Island to the port of Christchurch. We had to go through a narrow passage to get to the docks. When we were tied up we were allowed to go ashore. There were lots of people watching this ship from America and the seamen as they tied up to the dock. Most of us were invited to different homes. I was invited to the home of a teen age girl for a home cooked meal. I believe that all the seamen were treated the same way. The girls parents had prepared a huge meal probably used their entire weeks rations. The next day I had a couple of hours off so she took me into town. I saw an ice cream parlor and ordered a strawberry malt. The lady looked at me kind of funny and said, "the malts the flavor aint it?" When I returned the girl to her home her parents wished me well. I said I had to leave and their reply was, "give it a go yank." We were taking back wool, enough to fill the entire ship. We were ready to leave but a storm was out at sea so we decided to wait till things calmed down. The storm was so rough that it kept breaking our mooring lines. We spent the night and all the next day splicing the lines together. When the storm had subsided we headed out to sea. What we didn't know was that the pounding the ship got as it kept hitting the dock had split a seam in the bow. The ship was slowly taking on water. We were headed to the Port at San Pedro. When we were about half way home we started rigging the heavy gear so it would be ready for off loading in port. The ship was

123

taking on water and the wool was soaking it up we were starting to list on the port side. Rigging the jumbo bomb messed up the compass and for some reason the sextant wasn't working right, probably because there always seemed to be a cloud covering. We navigated by the stars when we could see them. When we first spotted land we saw some men in a fishing boat. The land did not correspond with the maps we were looking at. The captain using a blow horn asked the fishermen where we were. They did not understand him. One of the crew was originally from Mexico and could talk with the men. We were off the coast of Mexico near La Paz. We headed north towards San Pedro. Our ship was listing hard on the port side. As we were passing in the area of San Diego we first heard explosions quite a ways away from us. We looked close in the direction of the noise and saw a navy ship off in the distance. Looking in the opposite direction when we heard an explosion. Using binoculars we could see a target for the navy. Here we were sailing between the navy ship and its target. To our amazement we were not challenged until we were close to our destination. By this time the gunnel on the port side was almost under water. I was glad to be in the good old U. S. A. at last. I didn't go home I drove my car straight to San Francisco and put it in storage in a garage.

I headed for the union hall and was told I could get a ship that day. I signed on the S. S. Portmart as soon as I could get there. We were headed for the South Pacific and had been at sea a little over two weeks when we were torpedoed. I was able to grab a may west and a Vacco life suit before the ship sank. We all jumped in the water and swam as fast as we could away from the sinking ship. That night a squall came up and during the night we were separated. The next day I had to relieve myself really bad so I unzipped my life suit which immediately filled with water and sunk. I at least still had my may west and underwear. Late on the third day a Navy gun boat and sub chaser arrived in answer to our s. o. s. We were separated from each other but were picked up one by one. When we were all together I learned that only one seaman had died. After being checked out in sick bay one of the navy sailors gave me a pair of pants, too big but at least I was covered. The Navy ships were returning to San Francisco after having escorted a small convoy of merchant ships to Hawaii. They were the closest ships to us when they heard our S. O. S. When we arrived in San Francisco and were cleared I decided to go home for a few days. I took time to buy some clothes that fit me, then got my car out of storage and headed home.

Driving home I wondered if I was doing the right thing by being in the Merchant Marines but I knew I was needed there.. On my way home I stopped at the airport in Lindsey. I thought it would be great to go flying in one of the small airplanes. The plane that was used was a by-plane with open cockpits. It had been used to train the Army air Force pilots but was now out dated. The pilot told me how to attach the harness that would hold me in. We took off and the pilot did barrel rolls, dives and steep climbs I sure hoped that my harness would hold me in as I had no parachute. I enjoyed every bit of it. When we landed he asked how I felt about the war and I said I would be glad when we won and it was over. He wanted to know if I had heard about the new airport that was built in Tulare for training the glider pilots for invading in Africa. I explained that being out to sea we received very little news. He decided to give me another ride for free. As we reached a safe altitude he pointed out the many small farms owned by Japanese farmers. Many of them had small white cones covering young plants. As I looked down I could see that the cones had only been used in certain places. They had arranged them so they made an arrow pointing to the new air field. After we landed the man asked me if I wanted to learn to fly as I had seemed to enjoy the stunts he had performed. I said, "I would but couldn't attend regular classes." He said, "That's O. K. just stop by between trips and I will instruct you." I reached out my hand and said,

"Deal." He took time to give me a quick lesson. I headed home to Porterville. I spent one week at home then headed back to San Francisco.

I signed on another ship owned by the Matson Line. We were headed for the Hawaiian Islands with supplies for the Army again. We also had several service men with us. A make shift housing had been set up for them on the forward deck. Things were fine for several days. We spotted no other ships or airplanes. It seemed like it was taking a long time to get there, I guess I was just in a hurry. Most of the merchant ships being used were built in the early 1900s and only traveled at about 6 knots an hour. It usually took about 3 weeks to go from San Francisco to the Islands. I used up a great deal of my time off to study navigation. I was making a habit of this and the officers respected it and helped me when they could. We were just a couple of days away from arriving when we saw 6 or 7 planes headed our direction. As they got closer we saw they had Japanese markings on them. The armed guard were alerted and had their machine guns pointed in their direction. When the planes were almost over the top of us the guards started shooting. We saw one plane drop a bomb but it missed us. The man on look out saw some planes coming from the opposite direction and alerted the Captain. I was about midway on the aft main deck and he called to me to alert the Armed Guard. I ran in their direction and just as I opened my mouth a bomb hit the side of the ship. Shrapnel went flying and just as I opened my mouth to yell one piece went in my mouth and broke a tooth off. The bomb did little damage to the ship. I think the greatest damage was to my tooth. I had a real bad tooth ache. I did see a couple of planes go down in the ocean. We headed on to Hawaii as there was no way we could look for the pilots and the other planes had left. When we arrived we were met by some Army officers to get a report from us. When we were almost finished unloading and all the tween decks had been removed we heard that we would be in port a couple more days before receiving cargo to take back to the States. The Captain issued instructions that we should work on cleaning the ship. One thing that needed doing was the guys and stays needed slushing. This meant they were to be coated with a colored grease to keep them from rusting. I was the only seaman that had ever been aloft and I was instructed to climb the main mast and hook up a bosins chair to the dummy gantlan. The top several feet has no ladder and the dummy gantlan had been removed. The dummy gantlan is a 1 inch rope about 3 fathoms long. It is threaded through a pulley just under what is called the truck. It looks like a ball on the very top of the mast. As I shimmied up the last of the mast and attempted to thread a new dummy gantlan through the pulley a longshoreman pushed the handle that controlled the winch. This caused the mast to shake violently and it left me hanging there by just my legs. I was up side down looking all the way down to the bottom of the ship. It only took me a second to right myself then come down the mast. The longshoreman was Japanese. he was arrested right there. The worst thing was that after I had settled down I had to go back up and finish the job so I could fasten a bosins chair to the dummy gantlan

Much to my delight the Mayors daughter was there that afternoon. She had taken the time to find out the names of the crew. She waited until we were cleared to go ashore She greeted me with, "Avohu aloha ohoie" and a big friendly smile and offered to take me to a dentist she knew. The dentist did what he could do as I would be there only a few days. He finally removed the rest of my tooth. We went to a ice cream parlor and got a milk shake as I didn't feel like eating anything else. I had a hard time sucking on the straw as my mouth was still numb. She asked me if I still wanted to look around and yes I did. She drove me to a remote part of the Island where the natives still dressed and worked as they had done many years past. She told the plantation owner about me and he gave us a guided tour. We spent a couple of hours there then she took me back to the ship. The Captain asked how I was doing and did I get to the dentist O. K. I was feeling much better and told him I would be all right. I asked about the ship. There had been a through examination and it was deemed to still be in good shape. The next day as the ship was being loaded with some more caskets the mayor's daughter took me on a tour of the Mauna Loa Volcano. I was amazed to see so much lava rock. The flow of lava extended out into the ocean. There were miles and miles of it. It was now time to return to the ship and get ready to leave. We headed back to San Francisco and just 2 days out we passed another ship during the day time. The Captains of both ships used the blow horns to identify them selves. The other ship had spotted no enemy planes. The weather was great all the way to San Francisco. As we were interring the harbor we had to go under the Golden Gate Bridge. This entrance to a port is one of the most dangerous in the world. This is due to the shifting under currents. The pilot that was to guide us in arrived in a small boat and climbed up a rope ladder to the deck. He asked for the roster of all deck hands including officers. He saw my name on the roster and asked for me to steer the ship into the harbor. After we had docked and been cleared I got my car out of storage and headed home. On the way I stopped at Lindsey to get another flying lesson. I was doing quite well. I suppose studying navigation at sea helped me a great deal in passing the tests. I headed for Porterville for a couple of days then went back to San Francisco to get assigned to another ship.

My next trip I signed onto a Liberty ship headed to the east coast. There were a couple of company building merchant ships for the war effort. They were called Liberty and Victory ships. These were the first ships that had the steel plates welded together rather than riveted like the older ones. We were loaded with tanks and other war equipment. It was a real thrill for me as we passed the Statue of Liberty. When we arrived we were instructed to anchor in the bay. We were informed that we would be there just a few days but we were allowed time to look around New York as long as we were back on ship by 10:00 P. M. A small boat would take us to the main land every day. This was new to us as we were never allowed so much free time. Five days later we headed to Murmansk Russia with 84 other ships plus Navy escort ships. This was the largest convoy I had ever heard of and my first experience on a Liberty ship as I had heard that they could split in to while on the crest of a wave. Three days out to sea a big storm came up. I was on the wheel that evening. I was having a hard time keeping the ship on course as the storm was hitting us and causing the ship to heave over on the starboard side. When I had the wheel hard over and could turn it no further I told the officer in charge that he should call the chief engineer to take care of the problem. The steering engine is controlled by glycerin in tubes from the wheel to the steering engine. There are two valves that can be opened and closed to correct the uneven glycerin on the back side of the penicle. The officer said that he knew how to take care of it. By this time we were in the trough between high waves. The waves were so high that a ship would crest over a wave then dive down through the next one and completely disappear under the third wave. The officer opened the valves but opened one too far and glycerin spilled out on the deck. He tried to make it to the speaking tube to call the chief engineer but he slipped on the glycerin and couldn't get up. As the ship rolled in the trough he would slide from the port bulk head then back to the starboard bulkhead. I could hardly keep from laughing. The rolling of the ship woke the Captain up and he headed for the wheel house. As he stepped in he too slipped on the glycerin and fell to the deck. I watched the two of them as they slid back and forth, the captain using his weight to make sure the officer was always between him and the bulkhead. He ordered me to the speaking tube but I replied, "Sir I am on the wheel." When you are on the wheel you

129

only leave when relieved or the ship is sinking. He then said, "I am the captain of this ship you will call the chief engineer" I replied, "yes sir." I managed to get to the speaking tube, called for the chief engineer but never made it back to the wheel. I slipped and landed square on top of the captain's fat belly. I got a couple of free rides before the captain pushed me off and now I was the one hitting the bulkhead from starboard to port. As I hit the deck I put my hand down and got it covered with glycerin, it had no smell at all so I tasted it and to my surprise it was very sweet. The chief arrived and threw down some mats so he could repair the valves. Luckily we did not collide with another ship. On our way there I think there were about 10 ships sunk, I never knew the actual count. The water was cold and when a ship was sunk the seamen were picked up as quickly as possible, if they were in the water just a few minutes they would freeze to death. In Russia I was surprised to see so many women sailors. We did not get to go ashore. but as soon as all the ships were unloaded and re-fueled we headed back to new York. When we arrived this time I was really happy to see the statue of liberty. We only stayed in dock long enough to refuel then headed back to the Pacific coast and home. I was glad to be back on the pacific coast where it was much warmer. I decided not to go home this time as I could see the need for supplies and the transport of military men. I reported in at the union hall and was instructed to go to the Matson Line office.. When I arrived I was greeted by a couple of men in suits. In a few minutes they started asking me questions about navigation. I must have answered them correctly as I was given a test for my third mate's license. I passed O. K. and was handed a card with my name on it, and in bold letters was THIRD MATE. OFFICER UNITED STATES MERCHANT MARINE.

I went to the union hall desk and showed them my officer's ticket that the Matson Line had given me. The man at the desk told me to have a seat and he would get back to me soon. I saw him talking on the telephone for a few minutes then he motioned for me to come back to the window. I was instructed to report to the Matson Line office at a different address for further instructions. I was given the new address and when I arrived I was greeted by an armed guard. He directed me to the office where I needed to report. I was told that I need not report to the union hall anymore and that if I wished I could accept assignment on a ship and if I chose I could stay on that ship as long as I wanted or was needed, I need not report back to the office. From what I had experienced the food was always good on a ship belonging to the Matson Line and the company seemed to care about the seamen. With my new officers ticket I went to a uniform store and purchased a couple of uniforms. I was soon assigned to the S. S. John C. Calhoun. We delivered troops and supplies to Hawaii. After unloading we headed to Maui to load canned pineapple for the states. I was able to buy a case to take home. We returned home with out incidence with the exception that we saw one rare white whale. I went home to deliver the case of pineapple juice to my Mother. I spent a few days in Porterville showing off my new uniform. Mom was a good artist and when she saw me in my uniform she drew a couple of pictures. I laughed when I saw them.

I headed back to San Francisco and was assigned to another ship One day as I was walking down the street I saw a couple of sailors from another country, as they approached me they saluted and I returned a very awkward and much surprised salute. I wasn't prepared for this. I guess I was going to have to learn to be on the look out for this sort of thing. I was told the ship would be in dock at least two weeks so I could take some time off. Good idea I'll go home and show off my new uniform some more.

After arriving home and sharing my experience as an officer I went to the High School to visit some of my teachers and show off my uniform. Mr. Robinson the band director asked me if I could join them that Saturday. A new air field had been constructed just out side of the city limits and the band was to play for the opening ceremonies. We were to meet at the school and get on a bus that would take us there. I agreed to go if I got to play the euphonium. It was a fun trip as I got to meet all the band players. There were two members from when I was in school that were also on leave after completing basic training for the Army. Olive Primo was working for her parents that owned the local five and dime store. We had a great time talking about the, "good old days" and bringing all the latest news about our selves. Mr. Robinson asked if I could come to band practice the following Monday and I agreed. Monday morning Mr. Robinson explained to the class that I was the only one that ever asked to play the euphonium. He was glad I did as I could read music and could fill in both trombone and baritone parts. He then told me to go see the principal. I went into the office and Mr. Young said that the English, American History and Public Speaking teachers wanted to see me. As I visited each class room the teachers greeted me warmly and told the class a little about me while I was in school. Both the English and Public Speaking teachers had fun things to say about me. The American History teacher told the class that she knew I had to work hard while in school and that she often sent my assignment home with me as I had fallen asleep in class. She went on to say that regardless of this I was now helping to make history and protect our country and she was proud of me. By the end of the week it was time for me to head back to my ship.

I was back on board the John C. Calhoun as we were going to head out to sea in a couple of days. We headed for the Fiji Islands to drop off supplies. On our way we stopped off at the Philippines. We saw where some of the horrible things done to U. S. Forces were done. One man pointed out to me a mound of dirt. This is all that was left of a soldier. He had been buried up to his neck, a small stick was placed in his mouth to keep it open. A row of honey was laid on the ground from inside his mouth to a nearby ant hill. This was so the ants would eat him alive. There were other things that happened like an area about 50 ft in diameter, dug down about 3 feet and a high fence built all around it. Prisoners were herded into this fenced area then it was filled with fuel oil and sat on fire. I was appalled and even more determined to help win the war the best way I could. Our cargo was unloaded and we were ordered back to the United States immediately. We never made it to the Fiji

Islands. When we were approaching San Francisco, Sparks called for the pilot to guide us in. The pilot finally arrived in a small boat that transported him. When he started to climb up the ladder and the small boat started pulling away he slipped and fell up to his waist in the water, He was able to grab the ladder and make his way up to the deck. The pilot was so drunk he could hardly walk. The captain ordered me to the wheel as I was the most experienced with the under currents. We made it in O. K. thanks both to my experience and the captain's encouragement.

Upon arriving in San Francisco we were not allowed to go on shore. There were sealed crates and other war materials loaded on board. We were then ordered out to sea. With all this going on we figured that we were on a highly sensitive mission. When we were out to sea for a few hours the officers were called into the Captains quarters where he opened our orders. There was another envelop that was sealed inside the first one. We were told this was for the captain only. We were ordered to the South Atlantic Ocean then on to Africa. The exact destination was in the sealed envelop for the captain. As we sailed further out to sea we were joined by other ships. With each shift change the captain left the compass course we were to follow with the officer in charge. In a convoy you change direction every few minuets, making a zig zag course. We were at sea a couple more weeks before reaching our destination. While ships were being maneuvered one at a time to the docks the navy did the best they could to protect us but every once in a while you would hear an explosion. As you turned to look you would see men either jumping from a ship or lowering a life boat or raft as the ship was sinking. I have no idea how many ships were lost in the three days we were there. I was too busy keeping things in order and trying to keep the men calm. I knew we were some place off the coast of Africa. It took us about 3 weeks to get back to San Francisco which gave me enough sea time to earn my 2nd mate certificate. I was happy to see the Golden Gate Bridge as we arrived home. I was glad when they told us we could take a few days off. I headed for Porterville but stopped on the way to do a little flying. I looked around and saw that there were no more cones pointing to the Tulare air field. When I got home I just wanted to rest and clear my mind. I did not wish to talk about the last couple of months. I took the time to work out my frustrations by putting a new roof on the house. I did not tell Mom or any one else what I saw. I said goodbye and headed back to San Francisco and the Matson Line office. I was immediately assigned to another ship.

We were on another trip to the Hawaiian Islands. The trip was uneventful and the crew accepted me even though I was younger than most of them. The Mayors daughter met me and was pleased to see my officer's uniform. Two more days of loading cargo of coffins and equipment needing repair and we headed home. When we arrived in San Francisco I was told we only had a couple of days off. I decided it wasn't worth the trip home so I just hung around the Embarcadero. While walking along the embarcadero by the water front I saw a couple of drunk longshoremen. They had a bottle of whiskey between them and it had only about one drink left. When one reached for the bottle they got in an argument and one of them took his cargo hook and planted it in the other mans head. I didn't want to look any more as two other men ran to stop the fight. When I reported in they gave me the address of a seaman and told to go get him. When I arrived at the hotel I asked about him and they gave me his room number. I knocked on his door and he told me to come in. He was still in bed and as I approached him he started yelling, "Watch out for the trolley lines" he repeated this several times. I had been told that he was a wino, so now I found out what a wino is like when he has been drinking. I encouraged him to get dressed and get his things. I helped him to go to the union hall and left.

At the Matson Line office I was informed that at the end of my next trip I would be eligible for a 1st mates ticket and as soon as I had my sea time in they would send me to the Mariners Officer training school where I would get my final training to become the Captain of a ship. They informed me that as soon as I turned 21 I would be given a ship to Captain. This had me excited and I was eager to sign on any ship they suggested. I didn't care what ship they assigned me to as it meant I was closer to being a 1st mate and a neat pay raise. I headed for the ship they sent me to and took my things to my quarters. Officer's quarters are mid-ship and the motion of the ship is much smoother. We met in the Captains office and were told that our immediate destination was the South Atlantic. All things seemed to be going smoothly and the other officers were very friendly, more so than on the past ships when I first got my 3rd mates ticket. The Captain had a false leg and one day I got brave enough to ask him what had happened. He told me that one day when he was much younger and not as careful as he should have been that he was standing next to a mooring line as the winch was pulling it in. The line wrapped around his leg and damaged it so severally that it had to be amputated. This is when he decided to go to Mariners school and become an officer as it was less dangerous, besides he could no longer perform the duties of a seaman.

TAKEN PRISONER

The weather was nice and everything was going along smoothly even though we had no escort. The seamen accepted me as I hoped they would even though I was younger than most of them. We had been at sea about 10 day when off at a distance we could see what appeared to be five ships. We could not make out which country they were from. They turned and headed in a westerly direction so they were no longer of concern to us. The next day without warning we were hit by 2 torpedoes. I was asleep in my bunk and the explosion sent me through the upper deck, several feet into

136

the air, I landed in the water on my left side. The impact broke a couple of my ribs and I had a head injury from being blown through the deck or perhaps from shrapnel. The next thing I knew I was being pulled from the water into a life boat. I had a doozy of a head ache and discovered that some of my hair was covering my eyes. I had almost been scalped on the right side of my head and my chest hurt. We looked around and saw a couple more life boats, then off in the distance we saw a large ship coming towards us. We thought it might be an American ship but as it got closer we saw it was a Japanese war ship. When they were close enough we watched in horror as they machine gunned all the other life boats and seamen. They put a small boat over the side of their ship and came over to us. They attached a rope from their boat to ours and towed us back to their ship. They hoisted us up in our life boat and with guns drawn took us into a room bellow deck and closed the hatch (door). There were no toilet facilities or water and the light was turned on for about 2 hours every day or when they were taking one of us away. When they saw the blood on my face and looked at my head they joked with each other and laughed. We were in there for about 2 hours when the hatch opened and an armed man came in and took a seaman out. We could hear him scream and cuss. After a while they brought him back. His hands were bleeding where they had cut them. He said they wanted information about the American Merchant Marines and tried to make him tell information that he did not have. After a while the armed Japanese man came and took another man away. Once again we heard the screams of pain. When they brought him back we saw he had been flogged with a whip. They took the other men out one at a time and we always knew they were hurt in one way or another. I was the last one taken to what we called the torture room. When they took me to the room they first looked at the blood on my face and my head and nodded to each other and I guess they thought I would be able to answer some questions. They sat me in a chair and tied me so I couldn't move then through

137

an interpreter they asked about the number of ships in the American Merchant Marines and I said, "I don't know." The interpreter said they would see if they could help me remember and then poured cold salt water on my head as they lifted the part of my scalp that was loose. I again said that I didn't know and the interpreter said, "no true, no true." They then took my right hand and put some thin pieces of metal under my finger nails. Again I answered, "I don't know." One man slapped me across the face, they untied me and returned me to the room. The men said they heard me praying out loud part of the time. That evening we got our one meal of something that smelled and tasted rotten along with a dirty cup of stale water. One of the seamen had a stub of pencil and folded up piece of paper in his pocket. Every time they brought us our daily ration of slop he would put a mark on the paper. They took the seamen out one at a time several days apart and tortured them. The last man could be heard crying out in pain. When they returned him to our room he looked at me and started crying. He explained that he couldn't stand the pain. When they asked him if there was an officer among us to which he replied, "yes" Next they wanted to know who it was and he confessed to us that he told them it was me. They waited a few more days and we thought they were probably taking us to a concentration camp. Finally they came and took me to the torture room. They brought in something that looked like a large vise, then loosened the rope on my left leg and put my foot in the device. They asked many of the same questions over and over again. Each time I gave a negative answer they would tighten the vise a little more. I could hear my foot being crushed under the pressure. When I had no answer for them they returned me to the room. A few days later they came and got me and again I was escorted to the torture room. This time they did not tie me in the chair but instead ripped my shirt off, tied rope yarn on my thumbs and stood me facing the bulkhead. Then they tied the rope yarn to a bar mounted on the overhead so I couldn't fall. They used a whip on me a few times then asked the same questions. Eventually they got tired of whipping me and returned me to the room. The men asked if singing had helped and wanted to know more about the song, "I've got a home in Glory Land." They could hear me singing it very loud between my screams of pain. I also quoted some scripture from the Bible I had memorized. My body was in shock from the head wound so I didn't remember a lot of things that went on in the room. Several days later we heard three loud explosions, the ship shook violently. The hatch to our room was opened by the explosions. We went up on deck, breathed some fresh air and looked around. The Japanese paid no attention to us. They looked confused kind of like they didn't know what to do. We found a raft and when no one was looking a couple of seamen lowered it and one man picked me up and we all jumped in after the raft. We were well away from the ship and looked back at it. The Japanese running around on it reminded me of a bunch of ants on a log in water. The ship finally sank and I didn't see any one getting off of it. I am sure they must have sent out a distress signal. There were a few rations and a little water on the raft and a fishing line so at least we wouldn't starve the first day or so. The seamen did their best to keep me shaded from the sun during the day and would get close to me at night to keep me warm. I noticed that the man keeping track of the days was again doing it. He said we had been prisoners for 63 days. We were able to catch a fish every once in a while. We would tear the fish into five some what equal parts so we would all have something to eat. It did rain every few days and we filled the containers stored on the raft so we would have a little drinking water. My head was bothering me quite a bit and every once in a while I wouldn't be able to see very well. My body still being shock seemed to dull much of the pain. We had been on the raft a couple of weeks when I noticed that there were only four of us. I asked about the missing man and was told he went crazy from the heat and stress and jumped over board and they could not save him.

They had tried to coax him back but he didn't even try. I could not keep track of how long we were in the raft and had not seen an airplane or ship. One morning when I woke up two of the seamen were trying to wake the third man but without success. Later in the day we held a kind of ceremony and he was pushed over the side and floated off sinking slowly as he disappeared from sight.

I remember very little more until a ship was seen approaching us. When it got close enough we could see it was an American Navy ship. They swung by close and we waved at them. They put a small boat over the side, came over to us and asked us where we were from and what had happened. After a very brief exchange of words they towed us to their ship where we were hoisted up to the deck. They were very careful not to hurt us as they took us to their sick bay. They checked us over then helped us get cleaned up as we were all very weak from our ordeal. Looking at us they knew we had very little to eat in a long time so they gave us some very weak soup. They had us check our pockets and had small bags for us to put our things in but the only one that had anything was the seaman with the piece of paper or some kind of material he could write on and a small pencil. They asked him about the marks and he told them the first set of marks were the days we were on the enemy ship and the second set were the number of days we were on the raft. They had a hard time believing we had been on the enemy ship 63 days and not taken to a P. O. W. camp. They then wanted to know how we had survived 65 days on a raft. The seaman told them we stared out as five survivors but two of them had died. It was several days before we reached San Francisco. Upon arriving we were taken directly to the hospital where we were once again checked over. We were all put in the same room and it was there I found out that the two men that died had been giving me their rations and had actually starved to death. I was told they were trying to save the kid which was me. On the second day we were visited by a man from the Matson line. He brought us our money and took our statements about what had happened. That afternoon a couple of doctors came in to see us. After examining us I heard them talking and one said that they should notify my Mother that I probably would last perhaps another three days. After they left the room I got out of bed, took my clothes from the closed, got dressed and left, I wasn't going to die in the hospital. I slowly found my way to the storage garage, got my car and headed for home. I stopped very often and got a bowl of soup or a milkshake. When I got too tired to drive I pulled over to the side of the road and took a nap. What usually took me about 7 hours to get home actually took me 3 days. I drove when I was awake, some times in the daylight and sometimes at night. When I arrived home Mom was very nice and asked very few questions. She let me sleep for a couple of days just waking me up so I could eat. I was feeling a little better each day but still had my headache and my eyes would cloud over every once in a while.

I was beginning to feel a little better so I very slowly started walking around the yard. As time went on I began doing some of the chores. Moms' cooking was sure helping me get better. As I did more I felt better and was slowly beginning to put on weight. It didn't take long before I could keep busy all day doing little things. Mr. Martin Backich came over and asked if I felt like helping him on his milk route. He was picking up 10 gallon cans of milk from the local small farms and dairy's. He had to make 2 trips a day so the milk was always fresh and deliver it to Tulare Creamery. I said I would try but not guarantee anything. The next day I got up at 5 A. M. and walked to his place. We headed out and he told me to get the clean empty cans from the truck to replace the full ones he picked up. He would get the full cans and load them. We did this for about a week then he asked if I would like to try a full can. The milk cans when full weighed between 128 and 132 pounds each. I picked up 1 can and struggled to get it loaded. Martin would pick up 2 cans. The cans of milk weighed about as much as me. I kept feeling better every day. Hard work and good food was good for me. Each time we made a delivery to the creamery I would get a quart of very rich ice cream milk and drink it. Within a month I could carry 2 cans although It was hard. Later that month he asked me if I would like to do the route myself and give him a day off. It took me a lot longer but I managed to get it all done. A couple of weeks later he told me if I would buy the truck from him I could have the route for myself as he had decided to go back to raising honey. I told him to give me a couple of days as I wanted to see if I could go back to sea. Upon reaching San Francisco I went to the Matson Line office. They were surprised to see me and had their doctor examine me. The doctor declared that I was unfit to return to sea. I returned to Porterville and took over the milk route. I met Vaudine, a cute girl about 18 years old at one of the small dairies where I picked up the milk. She could pick up two cans of milk and load them on the truck very easily. We went skating a few times but mostly rode horse back during the day. She wouldn't let me saddle the horse; she just picked up the saddle by the saddle horn, lifted it up and sat it down gently on the horse. She was really strong. We became pretty good friends and I stayed with the milk run until I weighed 115 pounds and thought I would join the Army as I felt very strong about defeating the enemy, besides I was still angry at the way we had been treated. When I told Vaudine she said, "Come see me when you get back, I may still be available but I won't wait."

A high school friend said that he would like to learn the milk route and he could spell me off when I wanted it. He did not have to work Saturday or Sunday so he would be free. He learned very quickly and this gave me an idea. I asked if he could take a weeks vacation and do the route. He agreed to this so I did some checking around and found out when the next exam would be for the army. I was in luck as it was just 10 days later. I told my friend and he was able to take the time off from his regular job and do the route. When I went for the physical I was met by the same doctor that examined me for the Merchant Marines and he immediately checked me off as 4 F. I went back home and continued with the milk route until I weighed 120 pounds. When I tried for the Army again I was examined by a different doctor, was accepted and given a date to report to the bus station where we would be taken to the camp and inducted. This gave me enough time to sell the truck to my friend and get my things in order. I visited all my friends including Vaudine and told them I would be home as soon as I won the war, which brought a laugh. Told Mom goodbye on the appointed day and headed for the bus station.

US ARMY

We were transported to the induction camp and assigned to a barracks. The next morning they got us up at 5:30 in the morning. We were given 30 minutes to shower shave etc. then assembled to go to the mess hall. As we headed in single file we saw a soldier going in the same direction, he was walking kind of funny. He had his legs spread apart and slightly bent at the knees with his arms out stretched like he was holding something. The sergeant in charge of us explained that the man was off his rocker as he was riding a make believe motorcycle. We watched him pull over to the side and park his motorcycle then go in a back door to the mess hall. When we were through eating we were taken to a different building where we were checked out for what we could do best. I was qualified for a foot soldier and truck driver. Our next thing was to get outfitted with clothes. The uniforms were definitely not tailor made. If they were kind of your size they were yours. They had trouble finding shoes for me and finally went to the officers clothing supply where they found 1 pair of 5 1/2 extra wide shoes. We were issued a stamp with the last four digits of our serial number and an ink pad. We stamped all our clothes with the last four numbers of our serial number. As the days went on and we became accustomed to the rigors of military life and we started getting the shots we needed. One time we were lined up single file to go into a building to get more shots. The walkway was narrow, and there was a counter on the right side. Behind this counter was a medic with a needle in his hand and on our left side was another medic with a needle in his hand. The two medics timed it just right so you would get a shot in both arms at the same time. In front of me was a rather large soldier, as he received his shots he just keeled over on his face. We would see the man on his motorcycle going from one place to another. One day we saw him go into a doctor's office. Each evening we would have mail call and many soldiers received mail. There were several that could not read or write. I was surprised to see this as I thought every one could read and write. I was often asked to either read or write a letter and was paid $5.00 each time. That was a lot of money from a soldier's paycheck. As time went on we learned more about the soldier on the motorcycle. The man finally got a section 9 discharge and as he was leaving he parked his motorcycle, showed the guard his discharge papers and walked out the gate. The guard called to him that he had forgotten his motorcycle and he replied, "you can have it now, I no longer need it." This was the last we saw of the motorcycle. Every morning after roll call the Sergeant in charge would take us back into the barracks and start with inspection. He would first check our foot lockers to make sure all our clothes were neatly folded and put away. The barracks Sergeant would take a quarter, walk to your bed and flip the quarter. If it bounced up about 4 inches you were O. K. If the quarter did not bounce you were ordered to remake your bed until the quarter would bounce to his satisfaction. Early one morning after inspection we were given a duffel bag and stencils and told to mark the bags with our last name and the last 4 digits of our serial number and put our clothes in it. We had to strip our beds and put the sheets and blankets in a pile on the floor, we were finished by noon. After lunch we were loaded onto a train to go to Camp Roberts for basic training.

Late that evening we arrived in Camp Roberts and had a very late dinner. We were shown to our barracks for the night. The following morning we were marched to the mess Hall for breakfast. We retrieved our duffel bags and gathered in a very unorderly manner to hear what was next. We were called by our last name and first initial and assembled into platoons. Each group was assigned a barracks. It was now time to start our training. The first order of business was getting us in shape, that is after we received our shots. I felt like getting an inoculation of one kind or another was a daily routine. After breakfast every morning we had to do exercises for about an hour. It seemed like we were always practicing marching in step. Now that the fun part was over we were issued M-9 riffles which weighed 9 1/2 pounds. The first area we went to was to teach us how to clean the rifle.

There was one young soldier (David) that had been raised by his mother and I suppose never heard a swear word. When the instructor would explain something he used many swear words. David would listen intently then when we returned to our barracks would ask me to explain just what the instructor had said as he didn't understand the language. We spent the following day getting instructions on the different positions we could fire our weapons from. The prone position was the favorite and the most accurate. Friday we went to target practice where we could try out our skills without any score being taken. Donald always hit the bulls eye, seemed he was a natural. We marched back to our barracks where we cleaned our rifles. Saturday morning was the first time we had riffle inspection. The gun was held in a certain position and an officer would come by, reach out and take it from you. My rifle did not pass inspection. This happened 3 weeks in a row. The platoon sergeant inspected it and saw that the barrel was pitted and would never pass inspection. After we were free for the afternoon the sergeant had me put my mattress on the floor. He spent about an hour teaching me how to flip the rifle so it wouldn't be noticed when the officer grabbed it from me and he would drop it. When inspection came on the following Saturday the officer grabbed my rifle and I flipped it causing him to drop it. This meant he dropped it he had to clean it. He returned it after a couple of days and I rejected it. So the sergeant had to inspect it. He also rejected it. Now it was the company Captain's turn to inspect. He also rejected it and I was issued a brand new rifle. The only trouble was that I had to clean the cosmoline off which was no easy chore. I learned to like that rifle as I could never miss with it no matter what position I used. From there on I passed inspection and could get a week end pass.

We learned how to use a hand grenade we were of course using dummy grenades. We would be given a dummy grenade instructed to pull the pin and run up to a fake building and toss the grenade in an up stairs window as we yelled Geronimo. I was as good as some and better than most. When my turn came I was successful in hitting the mark most times. After a couple of days of this we went to an area that was marked, "live ammunition." The sergeant instructed us to lie flat on the ground. When we were situated another soldier several feet in front of us pulled the pin and threw his grenade away from us. When it went off our platoon sergeant had a hand full of gravel and threw it so it would land on me. I looked at him and said, "boy it sure throws shrapnel a long ways." He just grinned at me and told me what he had done.

We were scheduled for war games. We marched towards a large grove of trees and there we were divided into two teams. One red team and one blue team, one platoon against another one. I was handed a B. A. R. (Browning Automatic Rifle) which was at least 5 pounds heavier than the M. 1 Rifle. The red team marched to the other side of the grove and at a specified time we were to attack them. We were using blanks instead of real bullets. I spotted a tree that would shield me and ran as hard as I could, positioned the B. A. R. so the bipods would hit the ground first and I threw myself in the prone position. The one thing I hadn't counted on was that I slid passed the tree leaving me exposed. I soon learned how to put the B. A. R. down on the bipods and position myself. On Friday when we were through with the games we marched 5 miles back to camp to clean our weapons. Jim always gave everyone a bad time when ever he could. He never seemed to pass inspection and would lie on his cot every chance he got. This day he fell asleep instead of helping to clean up. Jerry went to the mess hall and brought back a small pot. Jim had his hand hanging over the side of his cot. We put warm water in the pot and placed his hand in it. After a couple of minutes he woke up with a start as he was wetting the bed.

We had to learn how to use our Gas masks in a hurry. We would enter a building to examine things and sometime while we were occupied mustard gas would be released. We had to put our mask on in a hurry. When we went outside we were checked to make sure we were O. K.

We marched several miles to a target range that had moving targets. Donald was again good until they started keeping score, then he couldn't even come close to the bulls eye. Every time we marched back to camp after an exercise Donald fell way behind. He just couldn't keep up. A couple of weeks later I passed inspection and got a week end pass. I went into Paso Rubles to look the town over and take in a movie. On my way to the theater I saw Donald walking down the street in civilian clothes. He yelled, "hi come here I have something to tell you." I walked over to him, he looked around cautiously to see that no one was close then in a low voice said, "If you play your cards right like I did. You know never hit the bulls eye and fall behind on a march you can get out too." I replied, "See you around and good luck." After the movie I headed back to camp. People around there were nice. If they saw you sticking your thumb out for a ride they would pick you up and go out of their way to take you back to camp.

We were on our last week of training and were really glad to see it over. When Saturday rolled around we got a two week furlough. I went home to see Mom and my friends, had a great time. Mom told me my Step Father was in San Diego. I drove to San Diego, found him working in a dairy. I talked to him a few minutes asking him many questions then my feelings got the best of me and I beat him up using the many tactics I learned in the Army. I drove back home still feeling angry. At the end of the two weeks I went back to camp as late as I could and when I went to our barracks I was greeted by the sergeant who informed me I was assigned to cadre to train new soldiers as they arrived. Starting Monday I was to instruct barracks clean up including making their beds, storing their equipment and cleaning up the barrack for inspection. When they were finished in the barracks I took hem to the parade ground and had them pick up every thing that didn't belong there. Following this I would give them their exercises. A week of this and I was ready to do something different.

That Saturday we were told if we signed up for 3 years we could choose the combat theater we wanted if not we would be going to fight the Japanese. I was afraid of what I might do if I went to Japan so I signed up to go to the European theater for 3 years. I was given a 10 day pass and told to report back to get on a train. The train took us to the east coast where we waited 2 days before getting on a troop ship. As we left the harbor we all saluted the Statue of Liberty. Heading out to sea I could tell that a storm was brewing. The second day a few of the G. Is. were sea sick. The third day out, the seas were really rough. The ship would crest one wave, dive down through the next one and almost completely disappear under the next one before starting the roller coaster ride over again. Most of the soldiers were sick. A couple of us were not sick and trying to clean up the deck and hammocks but it appeared to be a loosing battle. While we were trying to keep from getting sick our selves from the smell. An officer from the ship came to the soldier facilities to see how things were going. He told us that the seas were so rough that half the crew was sick. With this information I thought that perhaps I could help. I went looking for our platoon sergeant and found him on the main deck with his head over the side loosing his last meal. When he finally looked around and saw me I explained the situation and thought that perhaps I could help with the ship. He told me that it sounded good but if anything went wrong with the ship the Army would get blamed for it so I couldn't do it and I headed to the troop quarters hating to leave the sweet smell of fresh air. The ships crew that were not sick had to do double duty for a couple of days.

We did arrive in La Harve France safely. We were taken to a large field where tents were set up. There were about eight of us per tent. We were there for a couple of days before loading us on a train to take us to Paris. We were again put in tents for a day before we were taken to another depot in the north part of Paris where we were transported to Germany. Trucks arrived to take us to the war area. The trucks were crowded with G/ Is. and our equipment and headed for Germany. On the way we would stop where there were buildings to sleep in. The trucks were fueled up and the next morning we headed out again. We eventually arrived close to Ingolstadt where we were to replace some troops that had been on the front line for quite some time. They told us about seeing Russian Soldiers coming out of their fox holes that were dug in the snow in the morning with no coats and very few weapons. If a machine gun nest was spotted they would link arm in arm and over run it. As one soldier was shot another took his place.

The squad I was in was picked to replace the squad that was the forward point. As we were getting close to the Germans we heard a loud explosion so we carefully hurried to that area. We saw several soldiers running away from where the noise was. As we got closer we saw a soldier lying on the ground holding his legs up as high as he could. We saw that his feet had been blown off by a land mine. One of our squad ran to get a medic while I put my thumbs on the pressure points of his legs. Another soldier took his coat and shirt off then proceeded to rip his undershirt in strips to use as tourniquets. And so began my experience with another enemy. When the medic arrived we headed on to scout out the enemy. We came to a small town that was mostly destroyed and carefully began our search for people, booby traps etc. The German army started lobbying shells towards the American Army and the American army returned the fire. This meant that shells were passing over us from both directions. Fearful that one might fall short we looked for a place where we would be reasonably safe. We spotted an undamaged door leading to a basement, opened it and with weapons at the ready headed down the stairs. Much to our surprise there were 9 Germans in the basement with their weapons aimed at us. They didn't want to get shot and neither did we. One German spoke a little broken English and as it ended up the Germans stacked their weapons in one corner and we stacked ours in another. The agreement was that if the German Army came the American soldiers would be prisoners and visa versa. As it was the Americans came so we headed out on point once again. We were quite a distance ahead of our troops when some one spotted what looked like a German helmet behind some bushes. We were looking for a way to sneak up on it. The Germans must have spotted us about the same time because there was a sudden burst of machine gun fire. I felt a couple of stings on my legs but kept going. We surrounded the machine gun and 3 German soldiers. All our men opened fire at the same time and evidently got all the Germans as there was no more activity. Our soldiers were there almost immediately and decided that it was a lone machine gun nest as no one else seemed to be around. I saw a medic and asked him for three bandages. I had looked at my legs and saw I only had small flesh wounds. I found a medic and got three bandages from him. We continued on towards the next major city. It took us several days to reach Augsburg and we had no further contact with the Germans.

We were assigned to the Flak Caserne. All of the buildings had considerable damage from being bombed. As we searched for booby traps and German soldiers we came to the motor pool. The building was severely damaged but it appeared that the basement was still in pretty good shape. One squad was ordered to search it. As they went down the stairs they saw hundreds of cases of what appeared to be some kind of liquid. They were instructed not to touch them without an officer and medic being present. There were no booby traps so the officer took one of the bottles and read the label. The label was in English and read, "Potato Schnapps, bottled for the American Army by the German Army."

We were all billeted in the one building that had the least amount of damage. There were enough rooms so we were assigned two to a room. We were issued 2 sheets and 1 blanket. It was cold enough at night that we threw our over coats over us. German prisoners of war were assigned to clean our rooms. I felt sorry for the man that cleaned my room. He was an American citizen but when he was in his early teens his parents took him to Germany to visit with relatives. They were not allowed to leave Germany. He was ordered to participate in the German Youth Activities. When he was old enough he was forced into the army. He was told that if he didn't go they would kill his parents. We had many good conversations but he didn't know where his parents were. I got his parents names and the last place he saw them and told him I would try to locate them when I had time.

I was assigned a 6 x 6 truck to transport weapons and ammunition to the front lines. The truck had seen better days, I think it had been used during the entire war. On one of my trips delivering ammunition to the troops I saw a plane

151

heading my direction. When I could identify it I saw that it was a German Messerschmitt. I immediately turned off the tuck engine, pulled on the emergency brake and jumped out. Luckily when the plane fired its machine guns I was in the clear and the truck had pulled into a ditch so the shots did little damage to it. The truck was hard to start but I finally got it going and headed out to complete my mission. On the way I saw what looked like an almost new truck by the side of the road and decided to check it out on my return trip. The next day the truck was still there so I stopped to examine it. It wouldn't start even though the battery was good. I removed the gas cap, found a long stick that would reach the gas tank and checked to see how much gas was in the tank. When I pulled the stick out it was dry. I put a little gas in the carburetor and about 1 gallon of gas in the tank. The truck started after a few tries. I found a rock and scraped the numbers off the bumpers of both trucks to remove which group they belonged to. I then exchanged the hoods with the military numbers on them. I emptied the rest of the gas from my two 5 gallon cans into the gas tank, I put the empty cans on the fenders made for the purpose, started the truck and headed back to camp.

When I had a few minutes free time I decided to go to the compound where the POWS were. The guards on duty warned me to stay away from the fence and especially look out for the guard dogs. One dog in particular was very vicious. As I was walking around I saw the dog they were talking about. I had always gotten along with animals. In fact I found I could control most dogs with my eyes and voice. This dog looked at me and snarled showing his teeth and his ears laid back. I wasn't about to accept this from a dog. I started talking to it and slowly approached showing the back of my hand. The dog eventually quit snarling and lifted its ears up in a friendly manner. It had taken me several minutes before the dog accepted me. When one of the roving guards saw me on my knees and the dog leaning against me he called to another guard that had a camera and had him take a

152

picture of the dog and me. The picture was given to the commanding officer who called me in and wanted to know what I had done to the dog. I explained that I have a way of controlling dogs with my eyes and voice. He didn't believe me and watched me make friends with another dog. This seemed to satisfy him and he gave me the picture. I had quite a reputation amongst the guards after that. I visited the dog every chance I got. We became good friends. In fact at camp there were three dogs kind of being cared for by different soldiers. There was the Guard dog, Mookey, Sarg and 2nd Louie. I soon became friends with all of them and would often take them for a walk. I suppose I was looking for true companionship and I seem to have found it in the dogs.

I only had to make a couple more trips to the front lines and was thankful when V. E. day came on May 7, 1945. I still had other trips to take as we now had to get repair items and supplies. My next trip with the truck was to Stuttgart with several boxes of shoes for repair. I was about half way there when the pillar block on the drive shaft broke just as I was crossing a bridge. This made it hard to control the truck but I was able to make it across the bridge before the truck wouldn't move any more. I was happy that it was summer as I sat there the rest of the day waiting for an American vehicle to come by so I could send word of my problem. That night I slept in the cab. The morning hours were cold and I had nothing to cover with so I got out and briskly walked up and down by the side of the Auto Bahn, not getting too far from the truck. Around 9 A. M. a couple of German people came up to me, showed me an egg and pointed to the gas can on the fender. They also had a small container which could hold about a quart of gas. I gladly exchanged gas for the egg as I was hungry. The day went by very slowly with more Germans showing up with food in exchange for a little gas. I showed them the worn out shoes in the truck so they would know there really wasn't anything to steal. There were only two military vehicles that day and they did not stop for me. The morning of the 3rd day an officer stopped for me. I explained the situation and he said I should stay with the truck and he would send help. In the afternoon a tow truck came to my rescue. He took my truck and me to a camp in Stuttgart. I was informed that the truck would be ready the next day and I should let my outfit know what had happened. When I checked in with the 1st Sergeant he said he was glad I had called to confirm the call he had received from an officer. If I had not called in they would have listed me as A. W. O. L. the next day. My truck was repaired and I headed back to camp the following day. One day I was returning from a trip for supplies and some one took a shot at me. The bullet went through the metal and bounced off the floor hitting me behind my left knee. A couple of days later when I was on guard duty I was waiting my turn to stand at the gate. I laid down for a few minutes between shifts. I was on my side and when I woke up I couldn't straighten my leg. This removed me from guard duty and I was sent to the hospital. In the morning the doctor examined my leg and said I had lead poisoning. He had me lie on my stomach and with one hand straightened my leg then took his knife and cut the area open. All this with no pain medication. I had to lie on my stomach the rest of the day. A hot cloth was put on the area and a half hour later a cold cloth was put on it. This exchange went on all day every half hour. I spent the next day in the hospital then was sent back to my unit.

Back at camp they assigned me to the motor pool as a dispatcher and to monitor the Germans repairing tires. I made them aware that I was friendly and began learning a little German. This only lasted a couple of weeks before the commanding officer found out I could type. The company commander was looking over the records of the soldiers to see where to best place us. My records showed that I could type. I was told to report to his office. He informed me that I was the only person in the motor pool that could type that did not have a job that required typing and asked me if I would like a job where I would be required to type. I thought this would be a better place to use me. I spent one day at a typewriter writing reports but there was not enough work and a new job had opened up. I was sent to the office in charge of 8 German men. One man was a shoe maker, three men repaired type writers. One man built boxes to ship the personal affects of dead and wounded soldiers to their homes and two were assigned the maintenance and repair of all the cooking stoves for the division. They were hard workers and I learned some of the German language from them. I made sure that we had butter and coffee and every day they would furnish large pretzels which we buttered. We got along well enough that for holidays they would bring me a potted plant that was in bloom at that time. They surprised me by bringing me a hand carved plaque of the Augsburg shield. On the back were their names on a piece of paper covered with a plastic sheet. I liked it so much that they soon brought in more plaques. One showed the cymbal of the last king and queen of Augsburg showing their family heritage. There was also a hand carved Bavarian kitchen. Good momentous for me to bring home. A Major came to my office shortly after I was assigned to the job. He brought in some cartons of cigarettes and ordered me to purchase shoe leather on the black market. The leather was to be used in the repair of the shoes All I had to do was put the word out and Kurt was contacted and told tell me where I could get some leather. It wasn't long before I had the storage room filled with leather. Kurt always helped me pick the best. Kurt Schubert the shoe maker measured my feet and made me a pair of boots that would pass any inspection and a pair of dress shoes. These shoes were the most comfortable I ever had. The boots were a real plus as the boots we used for inspection were Army issue boots and were reverse leather so the rough part was on the outside, Hard to try and polish them. These shoes were made from the leather I had been able to acquire. Cigarettes, soap and candy were the items most often used to purchase things and the German peopled would do almost anything to get it.

Helmut Wassermann The lead typewriter repair man invited

me to go to church with him one Sunday. It was a fair sized church and had about 400 or 500 in attendance. I was warmly greeted by several people. I attended the church many more times as I was learning more of their language and could compare what they taught with what I knew. Much to my pleasure it was basically the same as I was used to. The clergy had to be very careful with what they preached during the war and were still being very careful. A group of the regular attendees asked me to go to an orphanage with them on a Saturday afternoon. As we walked through the orphanage a little girl took one look at me and with outstretched arms came running and yelling, "daedi daedi" (Pa Pa). I picked her up and she said 'wohin haben sie bin" (where have you been)? Every one was surprised. I guess I looked like her father. From there on every time I had some time off I would go see her. Those in charge eventually allowed me to take her to a park or just out for a walk. I often showed up in my German Leather pants I learned to love her as I would my own. I was told her name was Ingram. They did not know her last name. I continued visiting her until she was adopted. I was not given their name or address as she needed to bond with them.

Relaxed in Church yard

156

"Ingrid," Orphan Girl

My next assignment was to the special vehicle motor pool. My specific assignment was to build one good 10 ton tow truck from two that were in bad shape mechanically. I had to also move my personal things to a building that was closer to the motor pool. It was a large building, one end had a lot of damage from a bomb. The end where my room was had some damage with cracks in the ceiling. You could see moisture seeping through the cracks. I had two sheets and one blanket. There was no heat or hot water in the building. It was mid winter with a couple feet of snow on the ground. I used my overcoat to keep warm at night. It was cold enough during the day that the ink froze in my fountain pen as I was trying to write numbers of needed parts. I worked on the trucks about two weeks outside and was cold all the time. I became very ill and went to the dispatch office to get them to take me to the medical office. No one was on duty in the office so I filled out a trip ticket, it was basically a counter fit as I was not authorized to fill out the trip tickets. I went out side and found a P. F. C and ordered him to drive me to the doctor on duty. All was illegal but I didn't care. The doctor

157

examined me and told the driver to take the vehicle back that I was going to be admitted to the hospital.. My stay there was not the most pleasant of experiences. Penicillin had just been approved and it had to be administered by injection every three hours. I received a shot every three hours for thirteen days. The nurse on night duty had me lay on your stomach and bare my bottom. She then backed up a couple of feet and threw the needle like a dart. There were ten of us in the ward. One G. I. was African American. We found out he was afraid of the dark. Red Cross volunteers would come to see us every couple of days to find out if we wanted anything. One G. I. asked for some yarn for a project and they supplied him a ball of it. When the African American G. I. was in the bathroom the G. I. with the yarn tied one end of it around a leg of the African American G. I's bed then strung it around the room and handed me the ball. When the African American G. I. went back to bed he would first cover his head for a short period of time, then remove the blanket from his head. This was my signal to yank on the yarn. He would sit bolt upright then lay back down and cover his head. When his head was uncovered I yanked on the yarn again. This went on for several minutes until he no longer uncovered his head. One night of this and we decided not to do it any more. After getting out of the hospital I went back to the special vehicle motor pool. I completed the repair of one tow truck and was given the assignment of roaming the streets every night with the tow truck looking for American vehicles that might be in trouble.

One night a G. I. that was restricted to camp as he was always leaving the camp without permission and getting drunk on beer was once again up to his usual tricks. I saw the M. P.'s trying to catch him. He was running between buildings, came to a one story building, climbed on to the roof, ran across the building and jumped down to the alley. He had obviously done this before, only this time there was what the Germans called a honey wagon in the alley and he landed in it up to his neck. The wagon had a large tank on it to hold sludge pumped out of septic tanks. They persuaded me to put him on the back of my truck and take him back to camp. When I arrived at his barracks there was a group of soldiers waiting for him. They turned the fire hose on him even though it was cold with snow on the ground. The following evening I had to go to the Autobahn heading to Stuttgart and pluck a jeep from the branches of a tree. It was about ten feet up in the tree. I never did learn how it got there. It started to rain hard on my return trip. The sun had been shining all day and the pavement was warm so when the rain hit the street it became foggy. The fog was about two feet high, just under the headlights. I used trees, signs and what ever else I could see to guide me.

Another trip was to the Volkswagen factory in the Black Forest to pick up a brand new Volkswagen. The train ride there was not the most pleasant as I was in a chair car and the seats were made of wood with no padding. At the factory there was a big celebration as I drove the first V. W. Beetle off the line after the war. It was interesting to drive. The motor was in the rear and it had good traction even in icy places. It was slow going up hills as it had only 23 and 1/2 horse power. It did speed along at sixty miles per hour on the level. As I drove through, the townspeople would stare at this new black beetle. I delivered it to the motor pool in camp and returned to driving the tow truck.

I met many people at the church and was invited to their homes on several occasions. I always made sure that I had something to leave them as I was always fed lunch. Some times the food was pancake soup or beans always something they could afford. The clergy asked me if I had heard of the new program the U. S. wanted to start. The program was for German youth (G. Y. A.) and was to teach them games and help them understand the Americans way of life. I hadn't heard of it so they gave me the name of Colonel Haymacker. Colonel Haymacker explained that the program was to teach the youth fun games and constructive safe things to help them understand something besides war games. The Colonel had been informed how I used the sewing machine in the recreation room to sew on insignia and alter uniforms for other G. Is. He said if I was interested he would find a sewing machine so I could instruct the youth. I also asked if he could get me a record player. I would also have to use some of my free time to help. He had already been given a building for the purpose and hired two German women so there would be an adult there at all times. The building was of a good size and had small rooms along two of the walls. Saturday he picked me up in his chauffeur driven car and took me to the building so I could look it over. There were already a few youth just standing around looking for something to do. This looked like a challenge I would like to try so I was introduced as Sgt. Jones and given a set of keys to the building, I was given free reign to set up a program to teach basic English amongst other things. I took on the responsibility of teaching them the American way of life. Over the next couple of years I taught the young girls how to sew with a machine. Soldier from New Mexico taught square dancing. I purchased records from famous bands in America, Germany and Austria. I taught the youth the two step and they taught me the Polka and Viennese Waltz. It was a great time for all of us.

One evening while I was on guard duty I got a severe pain in my side. I was relieved from duty and the next morning I was sent to sick call. I was examined and sent to the hospital in Munich. After checking in I was taken to an x-ray room, strapped on a table so I wouldn't slide off. They turned me every way but up side down. After about an hour of this I was given a sedative and the doctor proceeded to remove a tumor from my kidney. During the operation the sedative started wearing off and I told the nurse about it. The doctor tried to make me forget about the pain. He told me he was going to get me court martialed as I had just peed on an officer. I stayed in the hospital another week while they took several more tests. I only weighed 138 pounds so they decided to keep me a little longer and feed me special food and give me exercises to make me gain weight. After three weeks of this I hadn't gained a pound. I was released and had to find my own way back to Augsburg. I hitched a ride on an Army truck. My commanding officer didn't understand why he had not been informed of my release so he could supply a ride for me. So much for the Army keeping track of every one.

I spent some of my free time exploring the historic places around Augsburg and the surrounding area. I was still required to deliver or pickup supplies from other towns. I also got to see many other places as I made deliveries or picked up supplies. Munich had at one time been a beautiful town with large church buildings and huge auditoriums where orchestras played and famous plays were put on for the Gestapo. You had to drive through the gate that was erected for the 1937 Olympics. In Stuttgart I was amazed at the almost total destruction. There was a hospital on a hill and across the Rhine River there was a castle. Interesting to tour the castle. People were living in it. There were dogs and chickens in the court yard. There was a high wall surrounding the castle with a cat walk up high where the warriors could look through holes in the wall and shoot arrows or throw their spears at the enemy. On one of my trips I was given the opportunity to tour the Dachau gas chambers. This sent shivers down my back but I had to see the whole encampment.

Franz Ostertag from church invited me to his home to celebrate my 23rd birthday. I suspect they had saved for several days as they had cooked a goose with all the trimmings. They lived in a building with three apartments. There was one room for washing clothes by hand and one room with a toilet. You didn't have to flush the toiled as everything dropped into a stream that ran below. Franz then asked me if I could take a few days off as he would like to take me to see the Alps. I arranged for a week off and we took a small narrow gauge train that had to make many tight turns, bending around the mountain side. The view was beautiful. We stayed with an elderly couple in their farm house. It was interesting as there was a Dutch door between the barn and the kitchen. The cows often stuck their heads in the open top part of the door. The couple had been married fifty four years and were still milking the cows and selling the milk and hand churned butter to the local people. We talked every night and they told me how it was before the war. They were also interested in life in America. During the day Franz and I climbed the Nable horn or took a ride in a gondola to the top where there was a restaurant. Every one was very friendly and interested in life in large towns both in Germany and America. Before our stay was over the elderly German couple gave me a beer stein that her parents had given them when they got married. The lady's parents had received the stein as a wedding gift when they got married. This meant that it was over one hundred years old. It was dull gray as it had so much dust on it. I took it as it was a gift, but really didn't care for it as it was so dull looking. When I got back to camp I cleaned it off and discovered it was beautiful with a picture of a female dog and her pups. The inscription said that with a good breed you receive beautiful offspring.

On Fog peak, "Nabel Horn"

23 yrs old

Franz explained that he had made arrangements for us to return in the winter for snow skiing. We returned to Augsburg and I had a warm feeling in my heart as I learned that most of the people near the Alps were Catholic and believed in God. The church I went to in Augsburg was a

163

Christian Church.

When I reported to the Sergeants desk I learned that I had a new assignment to the motor pool that had the responsibility of transporting goods to the military P. X. I was in charge of hiring drivers and overseeing the maintenance of the trucks. The first man I hired was Fritz who had been an S. S. trooper. Fritz had been forced at gun point to join. I had to get permission from the General to hire him and had to give a report once a month to keep him on the pay roll. I eventually hired five drivers. All the drivers had to back a semi truck down an alley and turn it into a door way. I must have checked out fifteen men before being satisfied with those I hired. The semi truck was hard to back up as it was a long wheel base truck with a short trailer. I had only done this for three months before I was also put in charge of the garage that did maintenance and repair for American officers and their dependents. This was a new challenge to me as some of the vehicles were the new automatic transmission cars and none of the mechanics had experience with them. The officer that had been in charge was due to go home. The garage had only been open for about four months and suppliers for all the parts were not yet arranged for. The officer that was in charge of me furnished cigarettes so I could purchase local parts. One challenge was getting broken glass windows replaced in a bus that been acquired to transport American children to school that had just been established. I was given the addresses of all the dependent children and was required to interview the parents to see if the children would be attending school. Once I had this complete I had to set up a buss route. When this was accomplished I had some free time to work with the German children in the G. Y. A. building.

I continued going to the German Church and was becoming very familiar with the clergy. One Sunday they asked me if I could give the sermon as the Germans would like to hear an American point of view. I thought about it for a few minutes and said, "I think I would like that. What do you want me to talk on?" They told me to pick my subject and be ready in two weeks. The church normally had 400 to 500 in attendance but could hold more. When the time came I wasn't ready for the enormous crowd, there were even speakers outside for those that couldn't get in the building. There were well over 1,000 people in attendance. I was a little frightened with so many people but soon forgot about them and concentrated on what I was saying. I spoke about God creating all people equal and that we should all learn forgiveness as Jesus told us. At the end of the sermon I got a standing ovation. I thought the people wanting to talk to me would never let me go. People came to me and on bended knee asked that I forgive them as they had come to harass the American combat soldier. I saw many people hugging each other, many with tears running down their cheeks. I do believe that many of them were surprised by what the Lord put in my mind to say. One man after asking for forgiveness told me I had changed his life.

Back at the motor pool (garage) I learned that the M. P motor pool had a hard time getting parts for their jeeps. I was asked to help with getting springs as they seemed to break very easily. Back at camp I still had to pass inspection every Saturday even though I had a room in town at the motor pool. I only went to camp once a month to pick up my pay. To pass inspection meant that I would have to go to the barracks every Friday night to make sure every thing was ready. I got by without having to do this as my brass belt buckle was polished and coated so it wouldn't tarnish, my shirts and pants were ironed and stitched so the buttons would not come undone. The inside of the creases were coated with a thin layer of wax so the creases would look sharp and stay that way. My foot locker that had my underwear was set up in the like manner. My personal things were stacked nice with a picture of my mother on top. I always passed inspection. One evening I was walking down town on a side street in my uniform and heard foot steps behind me approaching rather fast. I turned around and saw a man with knife drawn and heading for me. I used the technique taught me in the army and disarmed him. I doubled up my fist and hit him as hard as I could. He fell backwards hitting his head on the curb. I got out of there as fast as I could. Next day at the motor pool I heard that they had found a dead man lying on the street. It looked like he had been in a fight as there was an open knife in the street by his side. He had fallen and hit his head on the curb and died from the injury. A few days later I was walking down town in my leather pants and Tyrollean hat, a jeep with 2 M. P.'s in it stopped by me and one M. P. said, "High soldier," then laughed. He introduced me to the M. P. with him and told him that I was one of the good guys and he should leave me alone. He also explained that I was the guy that furnished them jeep parts. Colonel Haymacker was a regular customer and I often serviced his car, we became pretty good friends and he was pleased with my work with the German Youth.

Snow fell early that year so Franz asked me if I could drive us to the Alps which were 35 miles away. He wanted to teach me to ski. He first taught me to walk up a slight slope with the skis on, then slowly ski back down the hill. One time I was to follow his tracks and find him. He took a slight slope, I was a little slower than him his tracks disappeared down a steep incline. He laughed at me as I followed and tried to maintain my balance. The week end was over and we headed home. Monday things were back to normal. I took orders and dispatched trucks where they were needed, saw to the work in the garage and decided to spend a few minutes with the German youth. I was getting ready to leave when an American civilian approached me. He had orders with him that stated he was to replace me. I hadn't thought about leaving this position and it was a surprise to me until I realized that I was a couple of weeks over due to return to the states. My tour of duty was over with and I had not received any orders. I did my best to train my replacement. I saw Colonel Haymacker the next day getting fuel I went up to him and told him of my circumstances. The Colonel said he would try and find my records and I should report to him that Friday when I left the garage.

I gathered up my things and checked in with the Colonel, He had a room in the barracks ready for me and explained where it was, he also had a job for me until my records could be located. I was to take the week end off, gather my belongings from the other barracks and report to him Monday morning. I spent the time both with the youth and the church. On Monday morning when I reported in Colonel Haymacker had a job for me. The camp had been converted into a repair depot and I was to be in charge of stove and truck repair. I had a secretary, a man from Berlin. He was quite interested in teaching me High German as I only spoke Low German. He was also very good at making sure all the repairs were completed on time and parts were ordered as required. I only had to tour the stove repair shop and the garage. One day while walking down the row of the garage repair I heard a German tell the man next to him, "look out he speaks German." Never heard a word against the Americans after that. I got the feeling that Colonel Haymacker had made this job to give me something to do. Late in the week he called me into his office and said he had sent to the Pentagon for a copy of my records. Also the Army was checking out displaced people to see if they were truly the people that the Germans had forced to work in German factories or were they the ones that had come on their own accord and probably served in the army or held jobs at the German factories. He asked me if I would be willing to help interrogate the people. I was more than glad to help.

The following week I reported to the displaced persons compound and was given some ideas of what to ask. I returned to my quarters and put on civilian clothes. When I returned to the compound I discovered that there were at leas 200 people there. I was to live at the compound with them. I would walk among the people and listen to their conversation. I would approach some one and ask where they were from and if they would like to go home. I would suggest that perhaps they could persuade the American Army to furnish transportation and give them a small amount of money to go home. Some of them wanted to go home to family, some had no family to go home to and others were afraid to go home. I had to listen carefully as some tried to fool me. I was able to weed out some who had actually been in the Gestapo and one man who had been a high a official in the Messerschmitt airplane factory. There were two tents set up. I would walk with them to one of the tents depending on their answers and when they went inside I would give either a thumbs up or down. I spent the entire week talking to them. When I returned to camp on Friday Colonel Haymacker told me he would see to it that this would be interred on my records as soon as he heard back from the Pentagon. He then asked if I would take a special assignment for a few days. I told him I would be glad to accept any assignment he wished to give me.

He explained that when the fighting was over and the Germans surrendered that Germany was divided into four zones. Each zone was controlled by a different nation. The United Kingdom, Soviet Union, United Stated and France. The United States was in control of Bavaria and Russia had Berlin and surrounding area. In areas controlled by the Russians a high fence was constructed because the Russian soldiers would cross the dividing line and rob or harass the Germans in a neighboring sector. There were rumors of this kind of problem around Stuttgart and because I spoke German I could talk to the Germans and determine if there was such a problem. I was to go fully armed for protection. I was assigned a jeep and headed for the camp in Stuttgart. When I arrived I checked in with the 1st Sgt. and was assigned a room. I decided to get started immediately. I walked along the fence and sure enough there were signs of where people had dug under the fence or bent over the top of it. As I walked along the fence the Russian soldier on the other side would glare at me. There were several Russians walking on their side and none of them seemed friendly. I eventually came to an American Soldier on patrol. I asked him if he ever saw any Russian Soldiers crossing the boundary. He told me he had heard about it but had not seen anything. I spent the next few days walking around the houses in the proximity. When I would meet a civilian I would introduce myself and ask if they had indeed had problems. Some of them would talk to me once they found out I could speak German. Some of the people had been robbed and some hassled if nothing was found to steal. I wrote down all the complaints so I could make an accurate report. An Army sedan stopped beside me and the officer said, "What's your name soldier?" As I saluted I replied, "Sgt. Jones sir." He said, "Colonel Haymacker sent orders for you to return to Augsburg." The Colonel took my report and sat it aside. I had the feeling that the assignment was just another job to give me something to do while waiting for my orders. The colonel said my papers arrived and that I would be going home soon unless I wanted to reenlist. I decided to go home.

I went to the church as usual and explained to the people I talked to that I would soon be going home. They were happy for me but hated to see me go. I spent the week talking to the secretary and learning more High German. I also spent a lot of time with the youth. On Friday the Colonel called me into his office. he explained that each time my job became more demanding I was given another stripe. I had started out in the motor pool for supplying the P. X. stores as a corporal and was made a Sergeant. When they added the repair garage I was up graded to Master Sergeant, then with my assignment to check out the people in the compound I was again up graded to Top Sergeant This meant that when I mustered out I would receive back pay besides my mustering out money. I was a couple of months over due to go home and he had set it up so I would leave for the United States on the next troop ship which would be in three weeks. I spent my remaining days with the youth and all of them were sad to see me leave. There were hugs, hand shakes and tears on my last day. Sunday was my last time in the German church and much to my surprise it was announced in church. There was Apple Strudel cake, coffee and lots of well wishes. Karl Von Hauf came up to me with tears in his eyes. He had been one of the men that wanted to harass me. He had a souvenir for me one that he thought I would treasure. He gave me a big hug and handed me a package stating that I had helped him turn his life around. When I opened the package it was a micrometer. He explained that he had been a mechanic on Hitler's private yacht and this was one of the tools he used. Finally the day arrived for me to leave and I was all packed up with my souvenirs. We boarded a train for Bremerhaven and headed for home. In Bremerhaven I discovered that the Germans had still another dialect. It was easy to understand them even if you didn't speak German. I was glad to be going home to see my family and friends. When we arrived in New York harbor the Lady Liberty statue was there to welcome us home. I mustered out, received my back pay and mustering out money. I loved traveling on a train but wasn't prepared for the change in attitude of people. They were no longer as friendly and were too busy doing their own thing to welcome us home. In Los Angeles I boarded a bus for Porterville. My Mother met me at the bus station and took me to Grandmas farm house where she was living. Mom was still driving her 1937 Oldsmobile.

HOME AGAIN

I spent the evening with Mom and the next morning I went to the steamer trunk where I had stored my clothes and souvenirs from my Father and Grand Father. The trunk was empty and I asked my Mother, "What happened to my things?" She wasn't sure but she surmised that when my Grand Mother had passed away a lot of relatives were there and probably took them thinking that they belonged to my Grand Father. I then asked her for some of the money I had sent home but found out she had paid off the loan on the ten acres across the street and used some for Grandmas funeral then loaned the rest of it to my sister Georgia Lee and her husband Dick who had promised to pay it back. There should have been about $10.000.00 in the bank as I had sent home all the money I could while in the Merchant Marines and Army. The money I had sent home was enough to buy a small home. Now all I had was the money I had in my pocket. Broken hearted I decided to go to town, at least my car was still there and Mom had it serviced and ready for me. In town I expected to be greeted with more than just welcome home. During the following week I spent my time looking for a job but none was to be had. The service men that came home before me had taken all the available jobs. Georgia Lee invited me to Los Angeles and I could stay with them until I found a job.

I looked for a job a couple of weeks before going to an agency. The only job I could get was a service Station attendant, couldn't even get a job driving a truck. I accepted the job and with my first pay check I rented a small apartment. The service station was in Hollywood and many of the clients worked at the movie studios. They were all nice but I never did meet any movie stars. I went to church every Sunday and a man told me about a job with the United Parcel Service. I got the job and worked very hard and became one of the top drivers. I delivered the routes when some one was sick or off on vacation. I always beat the time allotted for a route until one day instead of opening a small gate I jumped over the fence. I landed wrong and injured my back. There were no office jobs available at the time so I had to look for another job as the doctor said if I stayed with the job I would loose my ability to walk and my feet still bothered me. So two years is all the time I worked there.

My next job was with the Rohr Aircraft Company. I drove a

semi truck transporting air craft engines to the local air craft manufacturers Special equipment was used to unload the cargo. There were a few other supplies like special tools etc. I also had to drive a bob tail truck to San Diego to pick up the engines from the Rohr manufacturing factory. I had to watch carefully as they would try to load the truck higher than the law allowed just to ship more engines. It was during this time that a new very large roller skating rink opened up in Culver City and I decided to try roller skating again. One evening while skating I saw this cute girl ahead of me (what nice legs) and skated up beside her. I skated beside her for a while and noticed she was a pretty good skater so when the next couples skate was announced I asked her to skate with me. We became a couple in the skate dancing lessons and it wasn't very long before we went to Las Vegas and got married. My job with Rohr meant I had to drive to San Diego very often. Cathy didn't like my driving there as it took several hours to drive both directions and she wanted me to be home and not work such long hours. I agreed with her as she was a lot of fun to be with. One day I had to stop at Williams Trucking Company to pick up some parts and was offered a job with better pay. I was assigned to Ducommon Metal Supply where I would haul steel to different companies.

My route took me to Glendale, Altadena Pasadena then all along the foothills to San Bernardino and back to Ducommun in L. A. The Jet Propulsion Lab in Pasadena (J. P. L.) was small at the time and was made up of several small buildings clustered together at the bottom of the hill. I seldom went there but knew where it was. Finally I had a delivery there and was curious about it as it was gaining a good reputation as the experimental lab for Cal Tech and was working on guided missiles for the Army. I had a load of sheet metal for the sheet metal shop. I asked the guard which one was the sheet metal shop and he pointed it out to me and advised that I should walk down and take a look as there was no place to turn around. I did as he said went back and got

172

my truck. I was able to back the truck in with no problem. While I was unloading the supervisor of the sheet metal shop called the supervisor of transportation and said, "You better hire this guy, he put a ten wheeled truck in where your drivers can't put a six wheeled truck." On my way out the supervisor Bill Kinslow stood in the middle of the road and flagged me down. The pay was less but I knew it was associated with California Institute of Technical College and thought maybe I could get some education so I accepted. I returned to Ducommom and the next day gave my 2 weeks notice. I started to work for J. P. L. June 15 1956. This was a new kind of work for me and I was excited and hopefully could get some schooling.

CHAPTER FIVE

WORKING ON OUTER SPACE PROJECTS

The transportation department consisted of the dispatch office, a garage large enough for a couple of trucks, a tire shop and the drivers room. In back was a trailer where our equipment was stored. When furniture or equipment needed to be moved we were given a work order. Often we had to take furniture blankets or rope and I found the storage trailer in a shambles. Furniture blankets were just thrown in and many of the lengths of rope needed to be spliced. I did not like spending my time in the driver's room just sitting around a waiting for an order so I started cleaning the storage room. I folded the blankets and started splicing the ends of the ropes that were in such a mess. I taught some of the other drivers how to splice and they seemed to enjoy doing something with their hands while they talked. I took it on myself to check the tires on the stored trailers and trucks. One time as I was reaching to the inside tire of a set of doubles I felt something sting me. As I brought my arm out I saw the black widow still hanging onto my arm. I went to the nurse's station and they put some Bactine on the bite. I waited for the effects of the bite but nothing unusual happened.

I soon had a good reputation and was assigned to the job of hauling explosives around the lab and from vendors as was needed and trucks with guided missiles to White Sands New Mexico. A couple of weeks before the semester started in the local college I signed up for night classes. I reported this to the records department. When the transportation supervisor (Bill Kinslow) found out about it he transferred me to the night shift. Luckily there was still time for me to change my classes to days. I continued to carry out my duties and maintained the storage trailer. I also made local deliveries and would pick up supplies. We had two way radios to keep us in touch with the dispatch office. When I was in the neighborhood of Cathy's parents I would stop by. Cathy's brother was usually there and very interested in the two way radio. Phil had enrolled in an electronics class at school bu t did not have the money to purchase the kits the teacher had requested. I would search the trash containers and retrieve every thing that looked like it was electronic. J. P. L. had a contract with the Army that required all unused items to be gotten rid of at the end of a project. This was handy as I often found unused items. On Sunday afternoon when we would visit Cathy's parents I would take these items to Phil. I wasn't sure if he could use them or not. Phil was very good at putting electronic things together and he ended up getting good grades in his class.

Our son Ed W. was born January 24, 1957 about 6 months after I started working at the Jet Propulsion Lab. Boy was this exciting. Cathy and I had been looking forward to this time as we definitely wanted children. Ed was a real joy to have around. There are many interesting memories of him. First as a toddler. Just before his 2nd birthday we had put up our Christmas tree and strung pop corn on is part of the decoration. Ed always got up early and one morning we caught him eating pop corn off the tree. The front of our house was at street level and the back was one story high. When he was a couple of years older some friends came to visit and the children were playing and decided to go out side. We had a freezer next to the stairs and I had put some snail bait on top of it thinking it was out of reach. Well young Ed saw it and got a hand full but refused to give any, "candy" to the other children They came running in to us telling us about his not sharing his candy. This got our

175

attention and I quickly discovered the problem. He had to get his stomach pumped but because he had not shared with the other children they were just fine.

The lead dispatcher interested me in raising Parakeets. He gave me a young one that we called Pete. Pete had French Molt, this causes their feathers to become unruly. This made it almost impossible for them to fly. Pete learned to talk a few words and one time while I was on a week long trip to White Sands a faucet in the bath room started leaking (just enough for it to drip). From that time on Pete would make the dripping sound all night. He loved to sit on my shoulder and if I was drinking something I had to have a glass of water ready for him as he loved to take a bath in what ever I was drinking. I often spent my lunch time with a Biologist, "Frank Morreli" and he showed me how to cultivate the culture causing the French Molt and went further with teaching me how to cure the problem. I wrote an article for the Bird Association of California describing the problem and how to cure it. Cathy and I were now thoroughly interested in Parakeets. We acquired a few more and began raising them. We interred many Bird Shows and eventually won several prizes including, "best in show." This was done by selective breeding in small cages. We also held offices in the local chapter an put out a news letter. We sold most of the offspring to pet stores and the birds actually paid for them selves and then a little more.

I made several more trips to White Sands and on one of these trips I was driving a semi with a guided missile on it. It was ready to fire with the solid fuel on board. I had to go through a special gate for vehicles with explosives. As I was heading to the launch area I saw several vehicles parked by the side of the road. Every one was standing outside looking up. I stopped my truck, got out and looked up. There was what looked to be a long cloud stationary in the sky. As we watched it suddenly started flying fast away from where we were. We then continued to the launch site. The following day we were called to a special room where we were debriefed and told that we saw an experimental aircraft that was using smoke to hid it from view it. It was the first flight of the vertical take off airplane. We were sworn to secrecy on certain items. The Jet Propulsion Lab developed a portable launch trailer to be able to launch a missile from any place a vehicle could go. I was positioned about 1/2 down range to be an observer. I was listening on my radio as the count down was made. When the words, "fire" were made the launch mechanism collapsed and immediately an alert was sounded and I heard them say, "we have a hedge hopper" meaning the missile was skimming along the ground heading in my direction. I quickly found a low place and looking over the edge I could see the missile heading directly for me. As it passed it was several hundred feet away from me. I breathed a sigh of relief and headed further down range to see if I could find parts of it. I helped locate the area for the first satellite dish. It had to be where there were few radio signals.

After I had completed some schooling I started looking for another position. The classes in rocketry, metallurgy and Algebra did me the most good in procuring another position, although biology was interesting. I worked in the transportation department for about 18 months before being given the opportunity to work in the Hydro Lab for Bill Williams. I learned to calibrate flow meters first

The United States was now in a race with Russia to explore outer space. Russia sent up the first missile, "Sputnik" and J. P. L. was working on Explorer 1. My first job was testing and calibrating flow meters. I was slow at this as I had to do a lot of math to get things right. One of the other men in the department loaned me his slide rule and showed me a little bit about how to use it. J. P. L. had a class on the slide rule twice a week for an hour. I took the class then purchased my slide rule. Less Peoples an engineer also helped me to learn more. He was interested in slide rules and had collected

177

many different ones. One day he brought his collection to show me. I didn't know there were so many different models. He had some that were round in shape. The largest one was about two feet in diameter, quite a collection I'd say. I also went to classes in metal working and Physics. Glad I was given the opportunity to take these classes while at work. One of the other men in the department was always complaining about not feeling well. After hearing his complaints for several days Bob, Chuck, Rat and I met him as he came in the door. We started telling him how bad he looked and after a few minutes of this he went home saying, "Now I am really sick." Yes I said that one of the men's names was Rat. His real name was R. A. Taylor, but he would introduce himself as Rat. Rat was due to retire and he gave me his Machinist hand book which I used many times. Explorer 1 was now out of the design stage. All the tubing had to be of exact dimensions. Just think I am now working on something that will go in space. I prepared all the tubing for Explorer 1 {Americas first Earth orbiting Satellite) then transported the satellite to the different departments for further work. I then was given the task of testing the Syncom fuel tanks in a special barricaded container. I had to pressurize them to 30,000 lbs. but most of them failed before reaching that pressure. We had new ones built that withstood the pressure then I placed them in ice water and tested them again. Next I worked for Dr. Elliot and Don Cerini. We were developing the, "Electro Hydro Dynamic Generator to be used on a long space mission. This was the first project I worked on that was an actual moving pat to be used on a space flight. It was very interesting to be working on a project that would be used to power a spacecraft. My first experience with a totally new item, something that had never been done before.

I met with Fred Gebracht and together we worked on the Hyperbolic Motor for the Moon Landing module (L. E. M.). Together we gathered the information, did some of the machining and finally I assembled the test unit and mounted it onto the test rocket module. There were other companies given the first try at it but could not produce one that would meet the dimensions and thrust requirement. The one we designed and tested met all the requirements. (This was the rocket motor used on the Moon landing module. The same one that brought the Apollo 13 Astronauts back to earth).

My supervisor Bill Williams requested that I accompany him to Dr. Pickerings office. Dr. Pickering was the director of J. P. L. at the time. The reason I had to go with him is that Bill Kinslow the transportation supervisor would not release me from transportation. As we went into Dr. Pickerings office I saw Bill Kinslow sitting there and I wondered what kind of trouble I was in. Dr. Pickering looked at Bill Kinslow and said I understand you want to keep Ed Jones in transportation. Bill Kinslow responded that I was the best driver he had and was interested with secret documents and the handling of explosives. Dr. Pickering looked at him and said I understand he is doing a good job where he is and I want you to release him to his new position right now. So my records were changed to reflect this. The next project that I worked on was the Electro Hydro Dynamic generator which could generate the electricity for a spacecraft that would be in space for many years. This was being designed and managed by Doctors David Elliot and Don Cerini. I did the assembly and testing with them there with me most of the time. Our tests were conducted with water and nitrogen and we could watch how it worked as it was mostly constructed of one inch thick Plexiglas. We could vie the separation of nitrogen and water and even saw a shock wave inside of a shock wave. In 1965 NASA began managing most of the projects. The technical people were to be reduced by about half as much of the work would be done by other companies and J. P. L. would over see the work and manage the programs. I was the latest one to be hired in the department so I was selected to be laid off.

Cathy and I took a two week vacation to the Sequoia Forest

where we found a nice camping area close to a stream that had lots of Trout in it. It was fun teaching the boys to live in the out doors and Ed W. learning to fish. When we returned home I started looking for a job. I saw an ad for a production engineer at Hycon. I knew nothing of the requirements but even though Cathy was skeptical I applied for the job and was hired. This was a new department that was being formed and we had to wait for a permanent location for our offices. We were temporarily placed in a trailer with no air conditioning so all the windows were open. We had no work to do and just sat around talking and swatting at the flies that would buzz around. I decided to go to the supply room and get some paper and other supplies to keep us busy. For some reason they also gave me a bottle of Eastman 9-10 which is a very strong glue that sets up immediately. To entertain ourselves we cut and folded small aerodynamic wings. We would then catch a fly with our hands and glue the feet of the fly to the wings. This was great entertainment. We spent three days in the trailer then were moved to our permanent location.

I was assigned to the K. S. 72 camera which was being made for the aircraft in Vietnam. This camera could take pictures from several thousand feet in the sky and read the license plate on a vehicle on the ground. We also made the Pan 55 camera which took panorama pictures. While working there Gary was born and he added a lot of spice to our lives. I worked at Hycon for three years working the last year as production engineer for the repair and retrofit department. The supervisor and I did not get along very well as he kept by-passing me when it came to salary raises and would often over ride my decisions even though I had been recognized for having developed the formula for the correct parts needed to retrofit the older cameras. While there I met Travis Brazil. Travis worked in logistics. Travis was born with only one arm but he didn't let that slow him down. Travis was not happy with his job and left Hycon to start his own business. Travis and I had become good friends. Our families often went water skiing and Travis learned to ski holding to the tow rope with one hand.

Our second son Brian was born May 26 1959. We now had another son that was a real joy to have around. When he was about 9 months old he decided to walk. He had not tried very hard to talk but we didn't worry as he was still so young, then one day when I arrived home from work he went running into his Mom and said, "Mama, Daddy's home." So his first word was actually a sentence. It was fun to watch him try to do every thing his older brother did. What a joy it was to have two sons. Both guys went to Church with us and as they grew older it often got confused over which one was which. We always made sure that all of us had dinner together and Brian very often kept us laughing all through the meal.

Gary was our third son was born January 7, 1962. Now our fun really started. We loved watching the boys grow and yes there are fond memories of him too. By this time we had an above ground swimming pool. I had built a deck around part of it so the boys would have something to stand on to jump into the water from. Gary loved boats and was often seen playing with his boat in the pool. One day he was so intent on watching his boat that he fell in fully clothed. Boy did he get teased. He also learned to water ski at about the age of four. He would go the neighbor's house about the time they were eating breakfast and even though he had already eaten he would tell them he was hungry and they would feed him again. We heard about this and informed him that he should not ask for food, only ask for water. We also told our neighbors about this. The next time he went to see them and they were eating he did not ask for food just said, "It isn't polite to eat in front of other people." I guess he was always hungry as he would go to see his friend Gene Ball at about lunch time and Rosalie would always feed him again. He grew taller than the rest of the family and now I have to look up to him.

When I left Hycon I went to work for Soderberg Manufacturing where they made aircraft lights. I was hired in as one of the managers. I was in charge of shipping and receiving, quality control and the design room. I hired Phil Smith, Cathy's brother as an electronic technician. Our work load increased enough that we had to hire more assemblers. On was a really nice young lady by, "Maria Hara" I introduced her to Phil. In 1970 our work load became lighter we began laying off workers. Eventually the managers had a meeting and it was decided that I was the one most capable of taking care of my family. I was given a severance check and left Solderberg.

Travis invited me to join him in painting and remodeling houses. I worked with Travis until June of 1972 and we were doing fine. Our families got together quite often. We went camping and one time and as always took our boat with us. Travis was successful in learning how to water ski. This was quite difficult as he had to hold the tow rope with one hand and adjust his balance that way .A job head hunter contacted me as Dave Elliot and Don Cerini wanted me to come back and finish the testing of the M. H. D. unit we had been developing in 1965. And so I began a new phase in my life with new challenges and responsibilities. I had to hire in as a contractor and would have to wait for an opening to be approved for the job. I was assigned to the group making and testing lasers while I waited. This was totally new to me and I had a great deal to learn about this new device. I worked there about three months before joining Don Cerini and Dave Elliot.

CHAPTER SIX

NEW CHALLENGES

My life as I knew it was changing with the raising a family, new responsibilities at work and church. As I checked in at J. P. L., I discovered that almost all the work had been completed on the Magnito Electric Hydro Dynamic Generator. All that was left was the final tests and this took a considerable amount of time. When the testing was over our group had a new assignment. J. P. L. had contracted with D. O. T. to improve emissions of the internal combustion engine. I was given a sketch of a reactor to build, it was our first attempt at a reactor that would convert gasoline into hydrogen. It didn't work as we wanted but it did give us some valuable information. The next sketch I received was a totally different design. It took me a few days to build it, then assemble two racks with the electronic equipment and control valves to control it. A 1974 Chevrolet was furnished us to do our testing. It had lots of horse power, the biggest engine that G. M. C. used in the Chevrolet and when driven would get about 9 miles per gallon. My supervisor, "Don Cerini" could watch all that I did out on what we called the patio as the door was Plexiglas. As I was completing the consoles I was joined by Dr. Cohung Chen. Cohung had recently arrived from Taiwan. He had a degree in Chemistry and it was thought that he could lend a helping hand. We had hoped that he could help us in our designs and experiments. I was to train him in Research and Development.

Due to the layout of the patio area the two consoles were about three feet apart and five feet from the test unit. One controlled the pressure and the amount of oxygen to be fed to the reactor. The other one controlled the gasoline pressure and metered the flow. Both consoles had a series of gauges and control valves. I had learned the correct mixture and pressures that we thought would give us the best results. Dr. Cohung was to watch me as I adjusted things and record the results and also learn to operate the equipment. Dr. Cohung was eager to get started and he was with me all the time. The only problem is that he was too eager. I would get one console set just where I wanted it and then adjust the other one. While I was adjusting the second console I saw the gauges going every fluctuating. When this first happened I thought something had gone wrong, then I looked over and saw Cohung playing with the control valves on the other console. The first time this happened I told Cohung, "Please do not touch the controls." We spent one entire day doing the same thing over and over again. The next day I talked to him and thought he understood. I was able to get the test going and was completing the fine adjustments when the gauges started fluctuating again. I looked over and saw Cohung messing around with the controls. I reached over and slapped his hand but this didn't stop him. Often when Cohung would change the controls we would actually burn up the reactor. This happened so much that others of our group started calling him, "Dr. Burner." Finally I had enough and asked Dr. Cerini what I should do. He told me I was doing just fine. The last time Cohung attempted to reset the instrument I walked over to him, physically picked him up and sat him several feet away, he looked at me and questioned, "me no do?" So I finally had his attention, I sat him down and explained what he was doing and how it ruined the tests. He never touched the controls after that, only recorded the readings on the gauges and the outcome of the experiment. We monitored the fuel the 1974 Chevrolet used, diverted 1/10 of the fuel to the consoles and ran it through the reactor. We then fed it to the carburetor and we not only improved the emissions but the car now got 54 miles per gallon and the emissions surpassed the requirements for 1998. The outcome

184

was sent to all automobile manufactures all over the world but none were interested. I had to use my slide rule quite often in calibrating. I had to also write reports on the item I was working on. My slide rule was slow and a new device had just appeared on the market, the hand held calculator. I purchased one even though it was expensive and it was worth it as it speeded up my work and reports a great deal. J. P. L. hired a new engineer to help us. Her name was Marietta Stephonoplis. We called her our Greek Goddess. She was not at all bashful. We only had one rest room and she didn't care if some one was in there or not when she needed to relieve herself or just to wash her hand. She was a real neat lady and we all liked her and kidded her every chance we got. She took it all good heartedly.

Cathy and I did not forget our vacations or long week ends. We purchased a small boat from a fellow worker. I had to do some repair work on it and the motor was in good shape. We often took friends with us to Lake Success or another lake to ski and do a little fishing on the week end. We sold our little boat and purchased a second used boat that was a little larger. I checked it over and everything was working fine. We headed for the local lake, put the boat in the water to try it out, things were working out as planned until the steering broke, a pulley had come loose. The boat was going around in circles. I shut the engine off and jumped in the water fully clothed. I finally managed to stop the boat from going around and around and with the use of a paddle and the help of our sons managed to get the boat to shore where I was able to repair the steering. Cathy started looking for a new boat and found one she liked. It was a tin hull and had even more room in it. When Gary was just 4 years old I fastened the children's skis together with pieces of wood so they would go straight I pulled Gary at 5 miles per hour and he did a great job of skiing. Cathy also learned to ski but she didn't care much for it, she was often seen driving the boat. We taught some of our friends to ski. Two in particular I remember. One was Travis Brazil. Travis was born with

185

only one arm and it amazed me how he could hold his balance. The other one was Willis smith that had M. S. and had little control of his legs. He put his hands in the foot straps and held onto the ski rope. He actually was skiing on his stomach. After work some of us would take our families and go to Hanson Dam for a few hours of fun. By the time we quit skiing all of us could ski on only 1 ski.

It was about this time that Cathy's father decided to take a trip to Canada to visit relatives. He came by our house and told us he did not want to take Phil with him as Phil was a lazy so and so. He said Phil only wanted to stay in his room and play with his radio. He didn't even want to go back to school and get his diploma. We agreed to let him stay with us for the summer. Cathy made an agreement with Phil. She would drive him around to find a job if he would go to night school. This worked out well so Phil found a job and got his diploma. He lived with us until he went into the Air Force where he was involved in radar. When he would come home on furlough he would come to us and sometimes bring a friend. When he got out of the service he rented a small place not far from us. Phil and Maria got married after he got out of the Air Force. Maria was a great addition to our family.

One of the men I worked with was Bill Rader. Bill had many stories about his experiences with a Boy Scout Troop where he was the Scout Master. Our son Ed had just joined local troop #591. There were only 7 boys in the troop and Bob Zerbal was the scout master. I volunteered to teach Morris code and 1st aid along with tying of knots in a rope. Once a month we would go on a camping trip and practice reading the compass and other skills the Scouts had learned. Almost all the camp outs were reached by vehicle. On one of our trips to 29 Palms we setup a compas course for the scouts to follow. While the scouts were following the course we walked over to where the end would be. As we passed an out house a little girl came out and yelled to her mother

186

"Momy, Momy I made it and only 2 breaths to." A few months later Bob Zerbal informed us that he was going to have to resign due to his work. I informed Bill Rader and he agreed to take on the added responsibility of another troop as the troops met on different nights.

BOY SCOUT DAYS

Bill introduced us to back packing and helped us build our back packs. I learned a great deal from Bill and the following year I accepted the Scout Master roll of troop #591. Cathy became involved as she joined the Mothers Auxiliary. The Mothers Auxiliary took care of the scout hut and the property surrounding it. They also helped plan special events held in the hut. The Boy Scout Troop had grown to 45 boys. I gave each scout an equipment list and expected them to use it. We practiced packing our backpacks at many of the scout meetings. On an outing If the Scout couldn't find an item I would dump his back pack on the ground and have him pack it correctly. We went on 1 back packing trip a month and once every two months I led the High Adventure Team on a more advanced trip. I taught them how to build a shelter and camp furniture using the fallen branches and trees. We became known for trail repair and propagation of trees at Henniger Flats and planting of trees in burned out areas.

On one of the trips to Henniger Flats the scouts were helping another scout to earn his Eagle Scout badge. This meant that the adults would do the cooking and clean up while the scouts helped propagate trees for reforestation and clean up the camping area. One young scout, "Gene Ball" complained about the food at every meal. I told him if he didn't quit complaining I was going to put him at the back of the food line. Naturally he kept complaining, so I put him at the end of the line. The food was cooked in two large pots. When it came time to dish out the food I reversed the line so Gene was in the front. As he approached the large pots he was directed to the 2nd pot. One of the adults scooped out what appeared to be soup while another adult reached in the pot with a stick and pulled out a sock. Of course Gene wasn't expected to eat this and I washed out his mess kit. He was given food from the 1st pot in his clean dish. He never complained after that.

Troop 591 was known for their repair work of trails and planting trees in areas where there had been a forest fire. One year we received trees from the Forest Service. Due to an emergency the forest service could not fly the trees to the planting location so they delivered them to us at the trail head. We had to bare root the trees and carry them up to where we were to plant them. There were two mentally retarded boys in the troop and they took most of my time. I told the senior patrol leader to over see the planting of the trees as the scouts knew how to plant the trees and how far to space them apart. When we got down off the mountain I learned that the trees had been planted correctly but they were planted in a great big 5 9 1, the number of out troop.

At one Camporee where the troops got together and competed, the Order of the Arrow was to conduct the camp fire. They had rigged up a rope from about 500 feet to where the camp fire was to be. One scout dressed like an Indian danced what he said was the fire dance. I knew better it was the rain dance. As he danced a burning arrow that was guided by the rope was shot towards the fire ring. Sure enough the fire lit but very shortly after that it started to rain, so his rain dance worked. Sunday morning our troop was asked as usual to give the, "Scouts Own religious Ceremony."

One summer Bill Rader and I took the most advanced scouts from the two troops on the Silver Moccasin hike in the Sierra Nevada Mountains. We would have to carry all our food as there was no drop off point. We had dehydrated food and this was some times augmented with fresh fish that the scouts caught. I had taught Brian to make a noise like a bear growling and he was to make the noise one night after we were in bed. Every time we would find a berry patch I would show the scouts the droppings from bears. When I saw other signs of the bears I would point it out. It took us 6 days to hike the trail. We had to carry our food as there was no place for a drop off. On the last night the weather was good so we just put our sleeping bags on the ground. Two scouts put their sleeping bags one on each side of me. After we had settled down Brian gave the bear sound and one of the scouts ended under me sleeping bag and all. Don't know how he did it but there he was.

The Scouts liked to go where we could take our canoes and maybe run white water. I had found the instructions on how to build a folding kayak. With this knowledge I suggested to the committee that we could build the kayaks and for our summer week long outing we could use them on the Colorado River. The parent committee agreed that this sounded like a good plan. We spent several Saturdays building the kayaks and the scouts painted them as they wished. You should have seen some of the various colors, the oars were painted to match. They were coated with a water sealer. The kayaks folded up nicely and several of them could be loaded on a pick up truck. We spent a couple of Saturdays at the local lake learning to row and steer the kayaks. When I felt the scouts were ready we made arrangements to make the trip to the Colorado River. We loaded the kayaks and our supplies in a couple of pick up trucks and the scouts were loaded in cars and station wagons. We headed for Glen Canyon Dam and put our kayaks in the river just below the dam. We had to carry all our food and equipment as there was no place we could be reached from the local roads. Everything was placed in the front of the kayak where it would be dry.

The first day one of the scouts got too close to a private dock and capsized. I helped him to get his kayak up straight but every thing was wet even though it was in a plastic bag. This meant that the food in the other kayaks would have to be rationed. In the afternoon we saw a ski boat pulling some one. It was going very fast and hit a large Sturgeon fish, knocked it unconscious. It took two men and a scout to pull it on board. It was still alive just stunned. That evening we built a fire and, cooked it and shared it around. That sure made up for the lost food. A couple of days later the Rangers contacted us and advised that we would have to make camp and spend the day on shore. There had been a flash flood and the dam would have to be closed above us to control the water flow. The water would not be safe for us to be on. We placed our bedding down where we could find a place for it, spent the night and the next morning began exploring the area. The scouts found a lot of fresh water clams where the water had receded. I showed the scouts how to prepare them and that turned out good. So now instead of having to ration out our food we could eat as much as we wanted. I explained how God was watching over us and was making sure we were saved and had enough to eat. The next day we continued down river. When we reached Lake Havasu we had enough time to explore the London Bridge where it had been relocated for an attraction for visitors before we headed home. We knelt down and thanked God for a safe and fun time.

One week after Mothers day we took our annual Mother outing. I would choose an easy trail, invite the scouts Mothers and have a Mother Son outing. The scouts would carry in every thing except their mothers personal things, do all the cooking and clean up. They even carried in some canvas to make a shield for the ladies latrine. They would teach their Mothers a skill or two. On one particular trip a scout from another troop came running to me and asked for help. Their Scout Master was trying to show off by climbing a cliff. What he hadn't noticed was that close to the top the cliff jutted out, he couldn't go any further and neither could he climb back down. I had the boys get the ropes out of their

190

packs, tie them together to make one rope long enough. On one end of the rope I tied a bowline loosely around my waist and the boys tied a small bowline in the other end. The boys fed the small bowline through the larger one and lowered it down to the man. Then the larger bowline was lowered down so he could put it around his waist. Using a tree to help secure the rope the boys slowly pulled the man up. The Mothers were really impressed by what their boys could do. Often times when we were on a hike I had to be ready when we stopped by a creek, took off our boots and put our feet in the water to cool off. I knew that sooner or later I would get thrown in the creek. The Scouts always laughed with glee. The worse blunder I made was on one camping trip. We had gone to an area where we could fire rockets. We went out Friday night and Saturday morning as I was fixing my breakfast I remembered it was March 15 and this was the 20th anniversary for Cathy and me. It was too late to do anything about it and I knew I would never be forgiven. Cathy and I stayed involved with the scouts and saw our three sons (Ed, Brian and Gary) earn their Eagle awards.

We were always involved in church, Cathy teaching the youth church group and I taught an adult class. I was chairman of the Deacons and later Chairman of the Elders. While chairman of the elders I received a call asking if our elders could serve communion at the local retirement home. I agreed and was the first to go. A lady played the piano and I led the singing then gave a short sermon in the fellowship hall. Two ladies appeared with carts, one had the loaf and the other the juice for communion. The lady's would stop at a room where the person was bed ridden, explain a little about them before I went in to serve communion. At one room they explained that the lady had actually died and they were able to bring her around again. She only remembered three things. Her name, the Bible and Communion. As I went in I recognized her as being a Sunday school teacher for me years earlier, what a blessing I received from this. There was always plenty to do with the church business. A friend of ours Bob Maclean and his wife Jan had studied to be missionaries in Indonesia. They had applied a received permission to go there. We formed a committee and I was elected president. It took quite a bit to get everything organized Bob and Jan have had a great deal of success. Cathy and I not only taught and served at church but helped with the maintenance of the buildings.

At J. P. L. we completed our work for the D. O. T. and I was loaned to a group working on removing sulfur from coal for the D. O. E. They were not being as successful as they wished and I was to use my mechanical abilities to help them. I designed the glass ware as a mechanic would do, not as a chemist. This helped some but the group supervisor had a difficult time getting his information across to the other chemists. He was from India and had learned Oxford English. He spoke very rapidly so it was hard to understand him. I learned that he had gone to school in Germany. I decided to speak to him in German. He would give his instructions and ideas in German and I would translate them. This worked very well and the project was completed on time. I was honored for saving the project at a celebration dinner.

With my newly gained knowledge it was decided that I should build a small chemical factory inside of a large empty building. The factory was for liquefaction of coal so it could be used the same as oil in boilers etc. This type of work was completely new to me and I had to do a lot of research. I had the factory completed so I could make a trial run. I used some of the coal that had the sulfur removed from it. Things went well and I had completed the project ahead of schedule. Another man was assigned to operate the factory after I had trained him. With my work complete there I was transferred to the group making and testing solar cells.

I learned how to grow the silicone billets which were then cut into very thin slices. These were put into a machine where the pattern for the solar cell was traced onto the silicone with a laser beam. The supervisor of the group purchased a computer. There was the monitor, key board. tape drive and a disk drive for a large 9 inch disk. A large wooden box by the side of the computer with lots of wires in it and an X. Y. plotter. A programmer was hired to program the computer. It was to test the out put of the new cells and chart the information on the X. Y. plotter. There was also a large solar simulator on a desk next to the computer. I was instructed to observe what the programmer did so I could do the testing. The programs were entered in basic language. I was fascinated by what he was doing. He was transferred after only 2 weeks of programming and the necessary information entered on the computer was a long way from being complete. Again I was put to the test as I had to complete the program to do the testing. It took me about 3 months to get things working right. I had to write the program so any of the engineers could access it, this meant that in basic a lot of the program was, "if this then that."

I walked every day at noon as one of the engineers was a recovering alcoholic and chose me to talk to. We would walk for about 45 minutes every noon with him doing most of the talking. I suppose I made the correct comments. Towards the end of the program he was transferred and I never saw him again. My name was given out at one of the manager meetings and I was contacted by several of the managers and offered a position with their group.

At this time I decided I wanted to be in a group that was working on satellites. I called the secretary and set up an appointment with the manager of the Gyro lab. I was greeted by the secretary and escorted in to see the manager. When I saw him the hair stood up on the back of my neck as he was Japanese and this was my first encounter with one after my being Japanese prisoner. I was surprised as I always thought I had good control of my feelings and had forgiven them. His name was Harvey Horowichic. Harvey treated me with up most respect and furnished every thing I needed and I learned to respect him. There were two things I needed to accomplish and that was to go to classes that taught soldering and mechanical assembly for spacecraft. I managed both classes with no problem. When I finished the classes I reported to the Gyro Lab and was greeted by Russell Allen who gave me a tour of the building and explained the equipment to me.

There were only five of us there and none of them got together during coffee break or at lunch time. This didn't set well with me. When I arrived in the morning I would make coffee. I would also bring in a dozen donuts on Friday. The charge for coffee was five cents and this covered the cost of coffee with a little left over. At morning coffee break I noticed that one of the engineers, "Joe" always had a piece of pie. In every lab there was a speaker and in the main room was what we called the squawk box. This was used so every one could be contacted. When Joe would get his pie out I went to the squawk box, pulled the handle and said, "pie time." After a few days of this the engineers would gather around the coffee pot and finally were getting to know each other. About 3o minutes before lunch time Bob Wendlant would put a heating lamp on the cold chicken he always brought in, so for lunch I would go to the squawk box and say, "the heating lamp is lit." This brought every one together again.

I contacted maintenance and arranged for a picnic table to be put under the trees out side the building. It didn't take long for every one to start bringing a lunch and we enjoyed many a good conversation, we really got to know each other. A blue Jay started coming around and we would feed it tidbits. I purchased some peanuts and the bird really went for them. The following year he brought his mate and their off spring. By now every one was feeding the birds. When the young birds were weaned the parents would chase them away but one young bird stayed in the area. We called him Spike. Spike was very brave and would land on the table. I started holding the peanut in my fingers and Spike would land on my hand and take the peanut. One day I held onto the peanut and Spike tried to take it. One of the engineers said peck him Spike and sure enough he started pecking my fingers right on cue.

We worked on many interesting projects like the Magellan, Topex Poisideon, Galileo, Ulysses and many others. Some were experiments for the shuttle and others were for the actual satellites. It was about this time that Phil (Cathy's brother) joined our group. He had been working for the antenna group. I helped develop the actuators that positioned the cameras. When the actuators failed on the Voyager spacecraft I took its twin and operated it under the same conditions as the one on the Voyager. It took several months of round the clock testing and it failed at about the same number of cycles as the one on the spacecraft. I took it apart and discovered that the particulates in the lubrication would separate from the liquid and bind up the very small gears. If I ran the actuator at half speed it would work fine. This enabled us to take pictures of Mars. We had to develop a reaction wheel for Galileo spacecraft as part of the craft had to remain stationary while the other part spun at 3 1/3 times a minutes. Phil was a great help in developing and operating the reaction wheel. His electronic knowledge really came in handy. I also helped with improving the electronics of Galileo main electronic board. Much of the original electronics had to be replaced as several new experiments were added to it.

I had to over see the addition of the building as we were adding new engineers and needed offices for them. Ted Iskenderian was newly graduated from college and I showed him around, set him up in the office I had prepared for him then helped him get started on his project. During the remodeling I designed a new Electro Static Discharge room for the assembly of electronics. I had done a lot of research and the new E. S. D. room became the fore runner of all modern electronic assembly rooms. I was one of 5 people in the U. S. A. to be contacted to advise other companies on the construction of their new electron assembly rooms. I remodeled an old test lab for another E. S. D. room and the NASA officials after inspecting it said, "I had made a silk purse out of a swine's ear," quite a compliment.

In addition to being in charge of the building I was given other assignments, was to design and build a portable unit that would help train the astronauts to control the boom on the shuttle. I learned about negater springs and other devices. The negater springs would remover the gravitational pull on the astronauts arm so he would learn to control the arm as if in space. I had to make spools for the negator springs so they could be adjusted for the different weights of every ones arm as no two arms are alike.

Our group continued to expand and share their ideas with each other. Ray Schliesman was one of the nicest people I ever worked with. When ever you had a concern or just wanted to share an idea he was always there with a listening ear. We numbered 27 and were recognized as the most productive group at J. P. L. We sure put the Apple 2E computer through its paces as all design and records were performed on it. Every Friday I would order pizza or gyros for lunch. Once a month we would go to a restaurant for lunch. One of the engineers, "Pete" remarked that what made this group so great is that we all believed in GOD. I had to agree with him but this made my move to another building very hard. Phil left our group and went to another section where he still works on electronics. He is well known and respected for his knowledge.

My office stayed in the Gyro Lab but most of my time was spent in building 98 where there was room enough for a new project. We had learned that the breathing air used on the shuttle did not have the filtering in it that the air that God created did. Without those filters if a person was a carrier of a disease, he could transfer that disease to another person. It was a long and sometimes tedious project. Through the directions of a Chinese chemist by the name of Jan it took more than 4 1/2 years to complete the project. I monitored the air and would induce different chemicals into it. I would add other chemicals to bring the air back to its original state. I never knew there were so many different gases in the air we breathe. I had to make the project do this automatically. When I was satisfied the unit was tested by several different chemical labs. The unit was then transported to the space station so the air would be the same as we breathe here on earth.

Gary and Jan presented us with our 1st Grand Son, "Cody" May, 1990. Now we had some one we could really spoil. I was thankful that I had an 8 hour job so we could see them often. It almost broke our hearts when the decided to move to Washington state to be with Jan's Mother and Sister. Jan's mother, "Ruth" thought Gary could get a good job there. So we began to make plans for my retirement and move to Washington to be close to them. We had planned on moving when I retired and had looked in many areas but their moving decided where we would move to, Gary and Jan made that decision for us. We took our vacation to Washington to look around. We did a lot of looking but found nothing that satisfied us. Cathy's good friend Polly had a cousin in the area we wanted to move too and her husband found a place for us in Puyallup, phoned us and Cathy made an offer that was accepted. We made a quick trip to Washington, checked out the house and Cathy immediately fell in love with it. so we signed the papers. We went home, started packing and I made arrangements for my retirement.

After a couple of truckloads we were finally in our new home. Cathy looked in the phone book and found a church that had two services. If it had two services it must be a good church. We immediately joined the Parkland Christian Church and continue going there taking part in many activities. The church was growing and eventually had four services. The name of the church was changed to Rainier View Christian Church and another campus was opened in a different location. We found the members of the church very friendly. There was one lady and her daughter that were especially attentive, Robyn and Renee Logsdon. It didn't take long for Renee to announce to us that she was adopting us as Grand [parents. We continue to follow Renee in her studies at college. We belong to the senior group, "Joy Givers." We meet once a month for a pot luck or a trip to a place of interest. Cathy and I still go to the parkland campus. Alyssa was born shortly after we moved to Puyallup. There are now 5 Grand Children: Cody, Alyssa, Chad, Logan, and Chaney. What a great family. We go to Vancouver, WA for Christmas and other festive occasions Thanksgiving is spent here with us. Both Cathy and I took the Master Gardner classes. I also joined the Western Cascade Fruit Society. I took an active roll and was soon elected President of the local chapter. Two years later I was elected President of the parent organization. Involvement in the local chapter meant that every year we would be involved in both the Spring and Fall fair. On holidays and special occasions we ship packages to members of our family. The young lady, "Kaydee Jones" that waits on us when we have something to ship now calls us grandma and grandpa. At the fair we met the Geigers and became very good friends with them. They introduced us the TAPCUG the local computer club where we learned quite a bit and also took an active roll, even taught some classes. The editor of the TAPCUG publication is Maggie Smith. Maggie has become an especially good friend. We get together with the Geigers once a week for dinner and table games

The Geigers followed us to California when we celebrated our 50th anniversary (what a fun trip). Richard and Betty drove their car and followed us. We were able to point out many things of interest to them. Richard was especially interested in the orchards and the cattle feeding lots. We spent each night in a motel so we were well rested and ready for the next day. When we arrived at Ed and Linda's house we found out they had every thing planned out. They had made arrangements for the entire family to meet at Joe's Crab Shack. There was lots of food and we had a fun time. When we left there we went to a photograph establishment where all of us had our pictures taken. Next day when we arrived at the Rosemead Christian Church we watched as our friends started arriving. They were neighbors, Church friends and people from work. All in all there were 50 guests. Stewart York the minister of the church said, "it isn't just an anniversary, it is a reunion. We returned home with warm feelings for our friends and family both in Southern California and Washington and we will continue to love every one for the remainder of our lives. We are very pleased that Renee and Kayde chose to join our family, we love them both.

I am at the time of this writing teaching youth about the Great Depression, World War two and Space Science. The teaching of the youth has inspired me to write this book and share my life experiences with family and all those that that have helped me and shown love along my life's journey.

GOD IS GOOD!